The raiders: desert strike force

D1448455

The raiders: desert strike force

Arthur Swinson

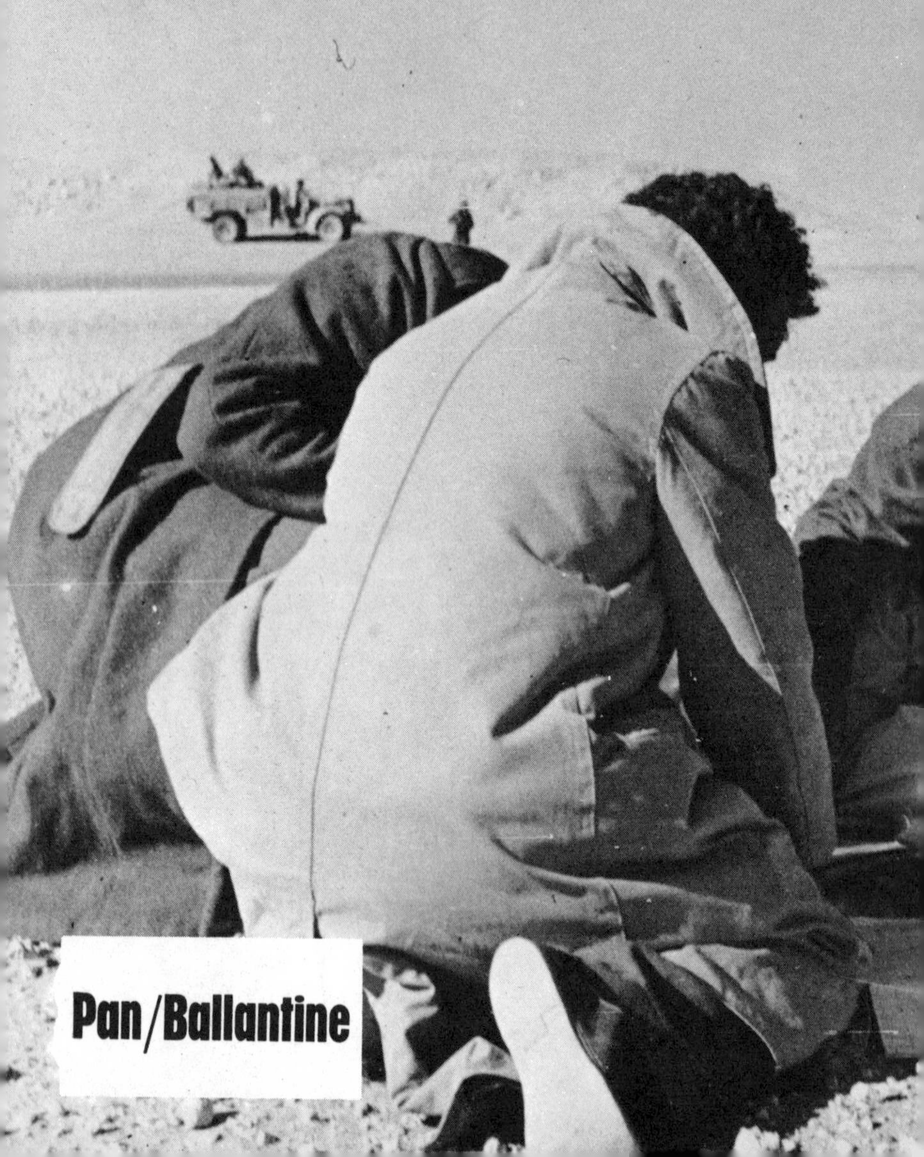

Pan/Ballantine

Editor-in-Chief: Barrie Pitt
Art Director: Peter Dunbar

Military Consultant: Sir Basil Liddell Hart
Picture Editor: Robert Hunt

Design Assistant: Anna Tryon
Cover: Denis Piper
Research Assistant: Yvonne Marsh
Cartographer: Richard Natkiel
Special Drawings: John Batchelor

Photographs for this book were especially selected from the following Archives: from left to right page 2-3 Imperial War Museum; 10 IWM; 11 Zennaro; 15 IWM; 16 IWM: 18 IWM; 20-21 Zennaro; 23 Associated Press/IWM 24 IWM; 27 IWM; 31 IWM; 32 IWM; 34 IWM; 34-35 IWM; 36 IWM/Zennaro; 40 IWM; 40-41 IWM; 42 IWM; 44 IWM; 45 IWM; 48 IWM; 49 IWM; 52 Zennaro; 53 IWM; 54-55 IWM; 56-57 IWM; 58-59 IWM; 61 IWM; 62-63 IWM; 65 IWM; 66 A N Wright; 68 Ullstein; 70 IWM; 72 IWM; 75 A N Wright; 76-77 IWM; 79 IWM; 80-81 IWM; 82-83 IWM; 84-85 Ullstein; 86 IWM; 92:93 IWM; 98-99 IWM; 100-101 IWM; 102-103 IWM; 105 IWM; 108-109 Camera Press; 110-111 IWM; 112-113 IWM; 114-115 IWM; 116-117 Camera Press; 117 IWM; 118-119 IWM; 120 IWM; 121 Keystone; 123 'Tobruk Commando' by Gordon Lansborough (Cassell); 125 Bibliothek fur Zeitgeschichte; 126-127 IWM: 128 IWM; 129 IWM; 130-131 'Tobruk Commando' (Cassell); 132-133 'Tobruk Commando' (Cassell); 134-135 IWM: 138 Associated Press; 138-139 IWM; 140-141 Bundesarchiv; 142-143 Zennaro; 144-145 IWM; 147 IWM; 148-149 IWM; 150-151 Bibliothek fur Zeitgeschiche; 152-153 Zennaro; 155 Bibliothek fur Zeitgeschichte; 157 IWM.

CONDITIONS OF SALE

This book shall not, by way of trade or otherwise, be lent, re-sold, hired out or otherwise circulated without the publisher's prior consent in any form of binding or cover other than that in which it is published and without a similar condition including this condition being imposed on the subsequent purchaser. The book is published at a net price, and is supplied subject to the Publishers Association Standard Conditions of Sale registered under the Restrictive Trade Practices Act, 1956.

Copyright © Arthur Swinson 1968

ISBN 0 330 24006 4

First published in the United States 1968
This Pan/Ballantine edition published 1974 by
Pan Books Ltd, 33 Tothill Street, London SW1

Printed in Great Britain by
Butler and Tanner Ltd, Frome and London

contents

Private armies

Introduction by Brigadier Peter Young DSO, MC

Wartime armies are made up of professional soldiers and of civilians in uniform. Neither civilians nor soldiers are necessarily warriors, for the former may regret their peaceful callings, while it is not unknown for the latter to prefer the dull round of garrison life to the excitements of campaigning. In truth all too few of either category make warriors, yet it is warriors that win wars.

This is a book about warriors, about men who, whether their background was civilian or military, had 'fire in their bellies', men who meant to carry the war to the enemy, officers whose audacity was tempered with originality, who were prepared to experiment and to throw 'the book' to the winds. The author pays tribute to Brigadier Bagnold and his Long Range Desert Group, who pioneered movement in the sand seas, until the desert, from being neutral, became an ally, albeit a fickle one, Without the LRDG the

SAS, to whose exploits most of the book is devoted, could have achieved but little.

From start to finish it is an astonishing story, from the moment when David Stirling persuaded GHQ to let him raise the unit, until the day when, after scores of hair-breadth escapes, his luck finally ran out and he fell into the hands of the Germans, winning a generous tribute from Rommel himself. The British the latter said had 'lost the very able and adaptable commander of the desert group which had caused us more damage than any other British unit of equal strength'. From any general this would have been high praise, but to be called adaptable by Rommel was praise indeed. Of all the high commanders of the Second World War he was the least affected by the siege-warfare mentality, which was the legacy of 1914–18. Rommel had seen some fighting on the Western Front, but most of his service had been in Roumania and Italy with mountain troops, whose work has been compared by his latest biographer, Ronald Lewin,[1] with that of 'a modern British Commando battalion or brigade . . .' Certainly the thorough professional who commanded the Afrika Korps was the very man to appreciate the exploits of the SAS even when they were raiding his communications and destroying his aircraft.

In 1939 the victors of 1918 took the field believing in a defensive doctrine that was to prove impotent against the *Blitzkrieg*. Thrust from the Continent in 1940 the British were compelled to become more enterprising, and took to raiding by way of showing that they were still in business. Thus the Commandos were born. It was from them that Stirling, Jock Lewis, Blair Mayne and others of his original band, came.

It fell to my lot to serve with the Commandos from June 1940 to January 1945 and for me No 3 Commando will always be, in the words of its first Commanding Officer, John Durnford-Slater, 'the greatest unit of all time'. In the autumn of 1943 we found ourselves at Termoli in a somewhat violent battle against 16 Panzer Division. On our flank were the survivors of the 1st SAS under 'Paddy' Mayne, a giant of a man, who was credited with having destroyed more enemy aircraft than any fighter pilot. I can only say that they inspired confidence. The Germans meddled with them at their peril.

Arthur Swinson's vigorous and fast-moving narrative successfully recaptures the atmosphere of enterprise and adventure, in which Stirling and his men achieved their amazing series of successes.

[1] Rommel, as Military Commander. Batsford, 1968, 63s.

The Major
comes to Cairo

In October 1939 Major Ralph Bagnold of the Royal Signals left England to take up an appointment in East Africa. Italy had not yet come into the war and the Mediterranean was open to British ships. Despite the tension of any wartime voyage, Bagnold could enjoy the autumn sunshine on deck and expect to reach Suez without incident. But, by a twist of fate, the ship was involved in a collision and put into Alexandria for repairs. Faced with a delay of some ten days or more, he decided to visit friends in Cairo, and had not been there very long before receiving a summons to the headquarters of General Sir Archibald Wavell, Commander-in-Chief Middle East. This great soldier was a man of few words and all he asked was: 'Would you like a job in my Command?' Unhesitatingly Bagnold accepted; for if Italy came into the war, Wavell would be fighting a campaign in Libya, in the Western Desert. And Bagnold knew more about this mysterious region than almost anyone on earth.

Running westwards from the Nile and southwards from the Mediterranean, the desert covers some 2,000,000 square miles. It is the most arid place on earth, and even a few miles from the coast there is rain only a few times a year. Further south not a drop may fall for years on end. Geologically speaking, the desert is composed not of sand but of a gritty dust, countless millions of tons of it, which since the days of the Romans has moved north swallowing ancient civilizations. The desert is not flat. In places the bare rock forces itself up to form low eminences, such as Ruweisat Ridge and Miteiriya Ridge; and to balance these are depressions, large areas of eroded soil, gouged like rugged scars. Some of these features have relatively gentle slopes, but others, like the Munassib Depression are contained by high cliffs. The

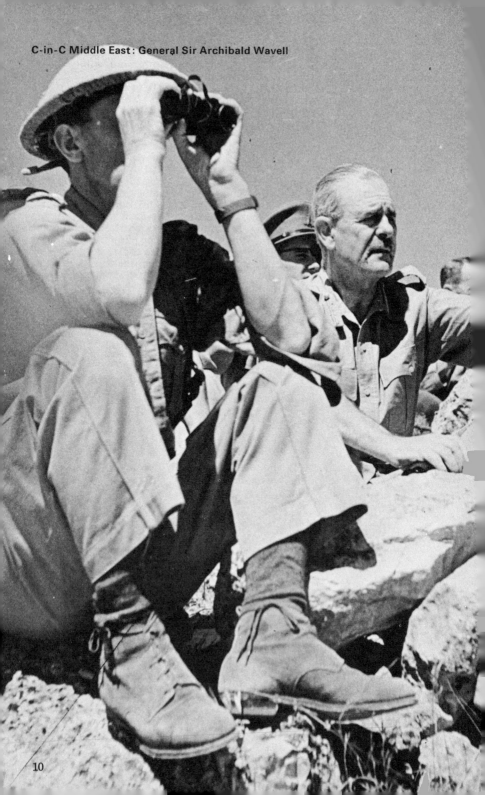

C-in-C Middle East: General Sir Archibald Wavell

The Italian Supreme Commander in North Africa: Marshal Graziani

largest depression of all, that of Qattara which runs south-west from El Alamein, occupies several thousand square miles, its floor 400 feet below sea level and consisting mostly of salty marsh. West of Qattara, pointing south like the forefinger and thumb of a misshapen hand, lie the Great Sand Sea and the Kalansho Sand Sea, known to the Arabs as 'the Devil's Country' and in previous times reckoned to be impassable to anything but camel trains. Within these vast features, oases do not exist. But, in addition to being dry, the desert is also very hot; away from the coastal strip, temperatures of 120 degrees in the shade are quite usual, and from mid-day onwards the sand shimmers in the heat haze. As Brigadier Lucas Phillips has recorded: 'Imaginary lakes, which the wandering Arabs call 'Devil's water', deceive the eye. Distant objects seem to float and move in space as the horizon becomes a quivering mirage.' With sundown there comes relief, though often at this time swirling sandstorms spring up, choking man and beast in a thick cloud of dust. The night glitters with a million stars, but the air becomes chilly, especially in winter, and before dawn the wind can cut like a knife. Altogether, the Western Desert is a strange, cruel place, where danger is ever-present, and even survival is difficult. It is a place which most men have always detested. But a few have responded to its fascination, have learned to know it and love it; and the leader of this select band between the Wars was Major Ralph Bagnold.

A regular officer of the British Army, he had been educated at Malvern College, and Gonville and Caius College Cambridge, and passed through the Royal Military Academy, Woolwich. In 1915 he was commissioned to the Royal Engineers, and served on the Western Front until 1918. In 1920 he transferred to the Royal Corps of Signals, and a few years later found himself serving in the Middle East. Taking a few enthusiasts with him, he began organising weekend trips from Cairo to the Siwa Oasis or to Sinai, and gradually became more ambitious until by the mid-1930s he was setting out on journeys of 6,000 miles or more, covering most of the

Italian infantry advancing

desert between the Mediterranean and northern Sudan. During these years he perfected the sun-compass, invented various devices for 'unsticking' cars from the sand, and amassed a great store of knowledge of all kinds. Despite his achievements, Bagnold remained a modest man, never attracting publicity; even to this day descriptions of him are rare and anecdotes almost non-existent. Neither his exploits, nor his subsequent publications excited any interest in the War Office, but fortunately the Royal Geographical Society gave him encouragement and support which enabled him to continue. By the outbreak of war he could move to any part of the desert and find his way back again; he knew the routes, the oases, the hazards. And being a professional soldier, he naturally

longed to use his knowledge against the enemy.

For some months, it seemed impossible for him to do so, except in an advisory capacity, but then on June 10, 1940 the situation suddenly changed, for Italy declared war and mobilised an army in Libya. Only 24 hours before this event, Bagnold had submitted to Wavell plans for a unit called 'Long Range Patrols' (later called the Long Range Desert Group) and on the 23rd these plans were approved. As the name suggested, the task of the unit would be to watch enemy movements beyond the Great Sand Sea and send back information vitally necessary to Wavell, as he prepared for the coming campaign. Hurriedly Bagnold contacted his old friends, the 'desert troopers' and asked them to join him in Cairo: Pat Clayton from Tanganyika, Kennedy Shaw from Palestine, Guy Prender-

gast, who was back in England. Within a month 30 officers and men had been assembled and the unit prepared for action.

The job was not an easy one, for stores were short and Bagnold could claim no priority. He persuaded a friend to print maps for him; borrowed theoddities from the Physical Department of the Government, and extracted sun-compasses from the Egyptian Army. Field-glasses and a thousand other items of equipment were either scrounged from the British population in Cairo, or bought for cash in the back streets.

But before the unit could even move, it had to have transport. Bagnold's pre-war journeys had been made in Ford 15-cwt trucks, excellent up to a range of 1200 miles but too small for the guns, ammunition, mines, and other equipment necessary for active service. Now he proposed to use 30-

13

The Long Range Desert Group gets the transport it needs: fully loaded 30-cwt trucks on their way to Desert Headquarters

cwt trucks fitted with special tyres, and as the army could not provide these, had to acquire them from the Egyptian Army and the Chevrolet Company in Alexandria. Many people thought they would be too big for moving over soft sand, but Bagnold was quite confident, and in the event he proved right.

The men were all volunteers, coming from a variety of units. Often they accepted a reduction in rank in their eagerness to join, captains serving as subalterns, and sergeants as privates. Three patrols were found by the New Zealand Army; their men were large, independent and, mostly of farming stock, and though ignorant of the desert, were quietly determined to master it.

But what did a patrol consist of? What was to be its complement of transport, guns and equipment? The establishment laid down by Bagnold as the unit formed was two officers and thirty men. These would move in 11 trucks, armed with a total of 11 machine-guns, four anti-tank rifles, a 37-mm Bofors gun, plus rifles and pistols as thought fit. In due course the patrols were found to be too big, and so were split into two, one officer and 15 to 18 men in five trucks becoming the norm. It is easy to see why this process came about: to survive every patrol had to contain a number of experts, signallers, mechanics, navigators, and it was only as his men became more proficient in more ways that the patrols could be reduced. Apart from men and armament, the trucks were loaded with three weeks' supply of water and rations, radio and batteries, sand-channels (for 'unsticking' vehicles), medical supplies, and other paraphernalia. And the trucks themselves were considerably modified, doors, windscreens, and hoods being removed, springs being strengthened, and special mountings being added for the machine-guns.

As the men and equipment arrived, but long before it was complete, Bagnold instituted a hurried training programme in cross-desert driving, navigation, signalling, gunnery, and the use of equipment. The initial exercises were necessarily simple and carried out near his headquarters in Cairo, which caused wags to dub the unit 'the short range desert group'.

However, rapid progress was made and five weeks after being given the go-ahead, Bagnold was able to report to Wavell that his command was ready for action. This was a remarkable achievement, made possible only by his dual skill as soldier and explorer. For once the British Army had put the right man in the right job.

Below: No spare water in the desert so beards are in fashion: Gunner Tom Kelly of Liverpool *Right:* In the desert it was courage and initiative which counted – not parade ground smartness: one of Kelly's mates

Into action

A glance at the map will immediately show the position in which Great Britain found herself during these early days of the war. To fight and defeat the Axis power, especially now that France had collapsed, it was necessary to mobilise the full strength of the Empire; dominions, colonies, and territories held under mandate. There was urgent need to bring troops from Australia, New Zealand and India, tin and rubber from Malaya, and oil from the Persian Gulf and elsewhere. Conversely, war supplies of all kinds, tanks, aircraft, ammunition, had to be sent out to the Far East. In short, communications between west and east were absolutely vital; and the Suez Canal, the link between the Mediterranean and the Arabian Ocean, assumed major importance.

British power in the Middle East was therefore firmly based in Egypt, astride the canal, and GHQ was sited at Cairo. Obviously, with the entry of Italy into the war, the Axis

strategy would be to seize the Suez Canal, so destroying Britain's communications and her power in the Middle East, and it was no accident that Wavell, generally considered the most able commander in the British Army at this period, should be sent to Cairo, with the urgent task of building and training an army.

What of the Italians? Their colony, Libya, lying immediately to the west of Egypt, and with a joint frontier some 800 miles long, running south from the Mediterranean, was a viable if not ideal base of operations. By the summer of 1940, facing Wavell's small force of 86,000, the Italians had built up an army of no less than 250,000 men. Included in this were nine regular divisions of 13,000 men each; three Blackshirt and two native divisions; and army and corps troops. The Italian Supreme Commander North Africa was Marshal Graziani, who had organised his forces into two armies, the Xth in Cyrenaica – that is in the territory immediately contiguous with Egypt – and the Vth Army in Tripolitania, to the west. After the fall of France in June 1940, he was at liberty to concentrate both armies for an offensive against the Nile basin, though whether he would do so, it remained to be seen. In any case, Wavell would be heavily outnumbered for many months to come and would have to use all his powers of generalship to save the situation.

It was in early September, after Pat Clayton had carried out some daring reconnaissance operations across the sand seas, that the LRDG was given its first big chance. After months of indecision, the Italians had now bestirred themselves and advanced across the Egyptian frontier, to Sidi Barrani. What was happening deep in the desert, and whether a right hook was being prepared in addition to the main coastal thrust, no one could say, and so Bagnold received his orders. The key to the situation lay at Kufra, the oasis lying to the south of the sand seas and so guarding the back door to Libya. Set in a depression and considerably below sea level, Kufra is remote, even by African standards, and has large stretches of water, fringed by palms. So ample is the water supply that for

Flamboyant but fast, an Italian motorcycle unit decides to move crosscountry

miles around lie Arab towns and villages, flanked by green patches of cultivation. The Italians had seized Kufra from the Senussis in 1931, so securing control of the inner desert, and had immediately begun fortifying the place, building up a garrison and military installations, and constructing airfields. Though remote, Kufra was in easy flying distance from Uweinat, where the frontiers of Egypt, Libya and the Sudan converge. At Uweinat, too, there was ample water apart from landing strips, and the two bases were on the route to the Duke of Aosta's forces in Abyssinia. So, in addition to providing a danger to Wavell's army, Kufra and Uweinat could be used by the enemy to cut off his communications with General Cunningham in East Africa and also with the French in Chad province, where the negro governor, Eboué, had boldly rallied to de Gaulle.

So it was on September 5 that Bagnold with part of his headquarters and W patrol under Major E C Mitford left Cairo for Ain Dalla, on the eastern fringe of the Great Sand Sea, then headed west for a spot dubbed 'Big Cairn'. This lay on the Libyan frontier and had been reconnoitred by Pat Clayton during surveying operations in 1932. Sited on a gravel plain between the two sand seas, the cairn was only five feet high but could be seen from a great distance. Gradually it became surrounded by dumps of food and petrol, as Kennedy Shaw ferried supplies from Ain Dalla, and Steele and Pat Clayton from Siwa. A few days later the patrols split up, Clayton heading for Tekro and the French Frontier, 600 miles to the south, Mitford for the area north of Kufra, and Steele back to Siwa for more petrol.

Mitford reached the Kufra-Jalo route and then a second route between Tazerbo and Marada without incident, though several men were sick from the heat and more than one became delirious. The water ration, incidentally, was fixed at six pints per man per day, ample in any other conditions, but the bare minimum here. When the sun was at its height, so Kennedy Shaw discovered, water became the only topic of conversation, and everyone had their own plan for making the

allowance go further. Some men would save up for a drink of Eno's in the evening, while others would put coolness before quantity and pour some water on to a tin plate in the evening, accepting the loss through evaporation.

On September 20 the patrol had its first battle, on the track to Kufra. What happened was that two six-ton lorries appeared, and in response to a burst of fire from the Lewis guns, their crews, consisting of two Italians, five Arabs, and a goat, were happy to surrender, and the patrol gained a haul of 2500 gallons of petrol and an official mail bag. As quickly as possible the prisoners were ferried back to Cairo, and upon their arrival the reputation of the LRDG was made. Rumours spread through the bars and messes that the unit had raided Marshal Graziani's headquarters. Wavell and his staff, though delighted with the exploit, were naturally more concerned with the accurate Intelligence reports which Bagnold submitted, and on October 1 the C-in-C sent the following letter:

Dear Bagnold,

'I should like you to convey to the officers and other ranks under your command my congratulations and appreciation of the successful results of the recent patrols carried out by your unit in Central Libya.

'I am aware of the extreme physical difficulties which had to be overcome, particularly the intense heat.

'That your operation, involving as it did 150,000 truck miles, has been brought to so successful a conclusion, indicates a standard of efficiency in preparation and execution of which you, your officers and men may be justly proud.

'A full report of your exploits has already been telegraphed to the War Office, and I wish you all the best of luck in your continued operations, in which you will be making an important contribution towards keeping Italian forces in back areas on the alert

Above: Italian troops on the advance towards Sidi Barrani. *Below:* Double machine guns at the alert: Corporal Bill Kennedy, Royal Scots Greys, in his truck

British infantry on the move, supported by light tank

and adding to the anxieties and difficulties of our enemy.

Yours sincerely,
A P Wavell.'

Never a man to rest on his laurels, Bagnold pressed ahead with new operations, his policy being to keep the Italians guessing; to confuse them to such an extent that they could have no idea where he would strike next. So, while Mitford headed for Ain Dua, Clayton attacked Aujila, 500 miles to the north. The garrison at this remote station considered themselves so secure that the Libyan sentry went forward to greet Clayton and was amazed when asked to hand over his arms. When the Bofors opened up, a great cloud of pigeons rose from the tower of the fort, and the Italians scuttled over the back wall to hide among the palm trees. A week later Clayton was back in Cairo, having made a desert journey of over 2000 miles in two weeks. Meanwhile Steele with R patrol had been across to Kufra, mining the road and destroying a Savoia S.79 bomber on the western air strip, together with some large petrol dumps.

Few military commanders like specialist units, knowing only too well how they can develop into private armies and absorb a disproportionate amount of men and material. But Wavell had faith in the LRDG from the start and immediately after its initial successes, decided that its strength should be doubled. So in December a Guards patrol was raised, half Coldstream and half Scots, under Michael Chrichton-Stuart; P J D McGraith raised a Yeomanry patrol from the Cavalry Division stationed in Palestine; and Holliman took over the Rhodesian patrol.

It was G Patrol which was allocated to the operation Bagnold had been planning in November. This was a raid against Murzuk, capital of the Fessan, in north-western Libya, in cooperation with the Free French. This month he had gone down to Fort Lamy, the headquarters of Chad Province, to confer with Colonel d'Ornano, the commander there, who was itching to get at the Italians. As he explained, a demonstration was needed that the Free French in the colonies did not lack the will to fight. D'Ornano was a tall monocled character wearing a burnous, and irresistibly he reminded the British of 'Beau Geste' and other films on the Foreign Legion.

Chevrolet 30-cwt truck
The basic equipment of the LRDG. There was never any standardisation of these vehicles, each being modified as its commander thought fit. Firepower was provided by various combinations of Browning, Lewis, and Vickers machine-guns. Normal range was 1,100 miles, carrying three weeks' supply of food and water

Naturally, as he understood, the operation would have to be a hit-and-run affair, for, even if the small Allied force took Murzuk, they could not hope to hold it for more than a few days. But if successful the raid would undoubtedly shake Italian morale and might even result in their moving troops from the front to the rear areas. Bagnold, who knew Murzuk well from his pre-war travels, explained that it was a great centre of Saharan trade, and an important garrison town and road junction. Apart from a small fort and a military aerodrome there was a town of about 3,000 inhabitants, and no doubt considerable supply dumps. The difficulties of the action, like those of most LRDG operations, stemmed from the great distances to be covered. Murzuk lay 1000 miles from Cairo as the crow flies and 350 from the nearest French post at Tibesti. Even if the patrols succeeded in reaching their objective unseen, there would still be the problem of getting away over the bare desert, probably harassed by air attack. However, the risks were known and had to be accepted. Planning went ahead with all speed.

Before the operation could be launched, however, there was a major development in the campaign: on December 10 Wavell had struck at Graziani and in a brilliant operation cleared the Italians out of Egypt and begun pushing them back across Cyrenaica, in the north-eastern corner of Libya. Thousands of prisoners were taken, and from some of these, detailed information concerning the lay-out of Murzuk was obtained and passed on to Bagnold.

It was on Boxing Day that the patrol paraded at LRDG headquarters. These were situated in the Cairo Citadel which stands on the verge of the desert, where the Muqatitam slope down towards the Nile. There is a superb view from the Citadel taking in the roofs of the city, and in the distance, the pyramids, on the edge of the Western Desert. The force commander was Pat Clayton, who also led T patrol (composed of New Zealanders), and G Patrol as already mentioned was under Crichton-Stuart, now facing his first desert operation. With him as navigator, there went Bill Kennedy Shaw, the Group Intelligence Officer. Just after 1500 hours Bagnold arrived to inspect the force which totalled 76 men in 24 vehicles, and then after a brief good-bye the column wound its way out of the Citadel, passed between the two mosques below then headed through the crowded streets of the city and over the Nile by Kasrel-Nil bridge, and made for the Mena Road. From here the column drove past the pyramids of Giza and by nightfall was 50 miles in the desert to the south-west. For the next two days the journey lay over the desert by the 29th the trucks reached Ain Dulla, a small oasis on the eastern fringe of the Great Sand Sea, then turned west. Now they faced the feature labelled by Clayton many years ago as 'Easy Ascent' – a great curving ramp of sand running up to the summit of a rock wall. Unfortunately the surface had been churned up by previous patrols, and the ascent was anything but easy. However, as Crichton-Stuart records, 'Just before sunset we filed over a narrow rock bridge between two deep gullies, a dramatic threshold to the Great Sand Sea and the back-door into Libya.'

Next morning as the party headed west across the 'Sea' the wind was bitterly cold and the men were glad of their sheepskin coats. Towards the horizon stretched line after line of dunes, some rolling but others razor-backed, and the trucks roared down the slopes of one to gain momentum for ascending the next. More often than not the momentum gave out before the truck had reached the top, and so it was a case of everyone clambering out to man the sand-channels. At this stage the drivers were not very skilled in selecting routes and the column covered only 60 miles. However, they soon learned, and on the tenth day the raiding force made camp on the edge of the Kalan-sho Sand Sea. Next day the journey lay over the Sea which stretches 90 miles in width, and camp was made in sight of the kilo posts on the track between Jalo and Kufra. By January 4 the column reached a spot about 100 miles south-west of Wau el Kebir, and the first stage of the operation had been accomplished. Murzuk lay only 250 miles to the west.

Now there came a pause, as Pat Clayton headed south to Kayugi to keep a rendezvous with Colonel d'Ornano; and Kennedy Shaw went south-east to reconnoitre the Terengi Pass, which, if things went wrong, might come in handy as an escape route. Meanwhile, the guardsmen of G Patrol filled in the time with some weapon training, PT, and arms drill to the amazement of the New Zealanders who concentrated on saving their energy and doing nothing.

By noon on January 7 Pat Clayton was back again, with ten Frenchmen and the petrol they had brought to the rendezvous on camels, through the passes of the Tibesti Mountains. The pessimists who had predicted that they would not show up were thereby confounded, and no one could doubt their determination to fight. Colonel d'Ornano, still monocled and immaculate, had with him Captain Massu, a somewhat uncommunicative swarthy figure, a subaltern, two sergeants, and five native soldiers. That evening (after Shaw had returned from his reconnaissance) there was a council of war, and all were agreed that the advantage of surprise should not be lost by an attack on Wau el Kebir, although it had a prison camp said to hold political prisoners. The main objective was Murzuk, and the plan decided on was to head there with all speed.

So next morning the trucks set off on a course to the north-west. Rapidly the country began to change, the sand giving way to a rough broken terrain of flat hills, and then a great plateau rose up, covered with gigantic black boulders. Beyond lay an escarpment, and here the column camped for the night, dropping down next morning to the plain, where fresh tracks could be seen both of men and camels. Then the barren desert returned and, fearing to lose the element of surprise, Pat Clayton ordered camp to be made early, in a hollow large enough to conceal the trucks. Murzuk now lay a single day's run to the west.

The latest information reaching Clayton was that the modern stone fort held a garrison of between 200 and 300 men, and possessed a wireless station. The aerodrome was defended by machine-gun posts. His plan was to cut off the fort from the aerodrome, contain it, then destroy the aero-

Above: **Difficult passage: negotiating the dunes . . . and** *below:* **'unsticking' from soft sand**

drome. Not possessing heavy artillery to knock a hole in the fort, the only hope was that the mere sound of the Bofors and 2-inch mortars would scare the garrison into flight. If, of course, they held their ground and called up air support from Hon, the base 250 miles to the north, then the situation would become difficult. But as always Clayton was optimistic.

By the morning of January 11, having camped some 30 miles off, Clayton, with Shaw, Crichton-Stuart and d'Ornano, wormed their way on to a ridge four miles from the objective, and studied it through field-glasses. There was the main road from Hon, disappearing into a thick belt of palm trees, about a mile from the city; the white dome of the mosque; to the left the wireless masts of the fort; then the roof of a large aircraft hangar. And stretching beyond to the horizon the white dunes of the Murzuk Land Sea. Like any commander, Clayton would have preferred a closer and more detailed reconnaissance, but as this was obviously impossible, he decided to go into action at once. Ballantyne, a New Zealander, would lead T Patrol less three vehicles against the aerodrome; while G Patrol with the three trucks from T Patrol would attack the fort. At 1230 hours after a brief lunch, the column moved forward, Ballantyne in the lead. As it reached the belt of palms, a solitary cyclist was overtaken who, on being hoisted on board, proved to be Signor Coliochia, the postmaster. 300 yards from the fort, the New Zealanders saw the Italian guard turn out, and despatched them with their machine guns before wheeling left along a track for the aerodrome. G Patrol under Crichton-Stuart then deployed, drove their trucks into the cover of broken ground, and after dismounting brought their guns into action. With the New Zealanders on the left and the guardsmen on the right, the small force was formed in a rough semi-circle, effectively cutting off the fort from the main road and the aerodrome. In the first moments, the Bofors hit a truck racing towards the main gate of the fort, and the machine-guns picked off small groups of Italians heading in the same direction. Massu and his troops joined the New Zealanders

who were now taking the brunt of th enemy fire. Sergeant Hewson, a Nev Zealander, was shot through the hear as he got his men into position Bringing up the Bofors to within 20 yards range, Crichton-Stuart ordere fire to be directed against the base o the wireless masts outside the fort but without success. Now it was the turn of Martin Gibbs, the Cold-streamer and second-in-command o G Patrol. Bringing his 2-inch mortars to within 200 yards of the fort, he began dropping his bombs over the walls. What he hit it was not quite clear, but before many minutes a column of black smoke began rising from the central block, followed by flames which soon obliterated the Italian flag. Before the fire had died down half an hour later, the garrison had brought their machine-guns into action, and the raiders found them-selves harassed both by these and snipers firing from the direction of the town.

Meanwhile T Patrol had launched its attack against the aerodrome. Not being able to spot the hangar immedi-ately after turning off the main road, Bill Shaw seized a Sudani who happen-ed to be standing outside a hut and dragged him on to the truck. The poor man was too scared to speak but this did not matter, as before the party had travelled much further the hangar came into view and the guards could be seen racing for their machine-gun posts. Luckily, the trucks were able to head them off, the guards sur-rendering, with one exception. He was shot dead. At this moment Pat Clay-ton's car came racing across the aerodrome, full of bullet holes. He had run into a machine-gun manned by a braver Italian than most, and Colonel d'Ornana had been killed at his side. By some mischance Clayton's gunner had jammed the Vickers just at the crucial moment and the only course had been to drive for cover.

However, Clayton began immediate-ly to deal with the hangar, bringing the Bofors into action. Before long an Italian appeared on the roof waving a white flag. The 20 or more defenders were now ready to surrender. Leading his men inside, Clayton found three Ghiblis bombers, and a portable re-fuelling tank. Rounding up the prisonrs he ordered them to pump fuel over he planes which, to his surprise he ound were armed with Lewis guns. At this point a message arrived from Crichton-Stuart to say that the garrison were still holding out, and Clayton decided that as his main objective – the destruction of aircraft and the hanger – had been achieved, he must now withdraw. The signal was a white rocket, but it had to be repeated several times before Crichton-Smith and his men saw it. This was about 1600 hours. The fire from the fort was now so heavy that it was difficult to get round his posts and give the withdrawal order, but then he was helped by a sudden dust storm which served as a screen. Soon G Patrol had joined Clayton at the aerodrome, where Crichton-Stuart reported one guardsman severely wounded in the leg, and three New Zealanders slightly wounded, apart from Sergeant Hewson who was killed. Forming a single convoy, the patrols returned to the ridge from which they had started a few hours previously, and here d'Ornano and Hewson were buried, to the sound of gunfire still coming from the fort. At sunset the raiders were driving southeast and a further 12 miles were covered before camp was made.

What had been accomplished? Three aircraft and their hangar had been destroyed together with installations and petrol supplies; 30 casualties had been inflicted and a number of weapons including four machine-guns captured. On the debit side were two killed and, as Clayton imagined, four wounded. But then Captain Massu pulled up his trouser leg to show where a bullet had been through his calf, leaving a neat hole. Cauterizing the wound himself with a cigarette, he had not bothered the doctor.

Next morning the force moved east again through the mist, the men casting a wary eye towards the northern horizon from where they expected hostile aircraft to come. But nothing happened, and after a while the column approached the village of Traghen which boasted a small fort. Here Clayton sent in an Italian prisoner with the threat that if the fort did not surrender within 20 minutes he would open fire. For ten minutes or more there was silence, but then shouts

were heard and the beating of drums, and a procession came out headed by the mayor and the town band. Solemnly the former announced the surrender. Inside the fort, Clayton and a small party found two machine-guns, rifles and ammunition, together with a vast quantity of documents. After setting fire to everything that could not usefully be taken away, the column made its adieus and headed across the desert towards Umm el Araneb, 20 miles to the east, and said to possess a larger fort and wireless equipment. Here the garrison was forewarned and had no intention of surrendering and after an exchange of fire, the raiders turned away. Now that the alarm had been given the wisest course was to hurry south towards Chad.

The trip, part of which lay over unexplored territory was not a comfortable one and in fact the country was the worst the LRDG had ever experienced. As Crichton-Stuart has said: 'From broken plateaux we crawled down into precipitous rock-covered valleys, only to find a way out with much labour, placing flat stones over the soft sandy patches between the stony going, and charging the trucks up the side one by one . . . It was wild and fantastic country, obviously impassable to motor transport . . .' On January 19 the column reached the forward French post of Zouar, set in a gorge never before negotiated by any wheeled vehicle whatsoever. Here Massu's fort towered above the native huts, and just before sunset the Senegalese guard turned out beneath the Union Jack and the Cross of Lorraine which fluttered from twin flag poles, and presented arms as G Patrol moved slowly through the gates.

At Zouar there was not only unlimited water to wash in, there was roast mutton for the troops, wine, and a seven course dinner for the officers.

The operation was over. But already there was a signal from Bagnold which read: 'Report at once how many trucks fit to join French in operation against Kufra.' The following day Bagnold arrived in person, then flew off with Bill Shaw for the French headquarters at Lamy. Here he held discussions with d'Ornano's successor,

Desert types: headgear optional, ?range essential

Colonel Leclerc. Both were agreed that planning must begin at once.

Leclerc was afterwards to become a great name, and it is worthwhile pausing to introduce him. A regular cavalry officer, commissioned from St. Cyr, he had been a captain on the outbreak of war. Fair, handsome, with a superb voice, he possessed a natural authority, and indeed 'Leclerc' was only a pseudonym, made necessary by the situation in occupied France. In fact, he was le Vicomte de Haute Coque. Wounded and then captured during the Battle of France, Leclerc managed to escape to a chateau owned by some relations. From there he travelled by bicycle to the Channel coast and then managed to cross to England. Having joined de Gaulle he was sent to the Cameroons to organise resistance to the Vichy authorities, and from here was posted to Chad. His troops were mostly Saras under French officers and NCOs, and all good fighting men, but his supply problems were enormous. Any old vehicle he could get hold of was cannibalised to provide parts for the guns and he was not too proud to comb the scrap heaps. His staff officer was Capitaine de Guillebon, a tall, lean and energetic officer who understood the Colonel's mind perfectly, and was to play a distinguished part in the actions to come.

For the Kufra operation Leclerc had 100 Europeans, and 300 native troops, with an armament of four heavy machine-guns, 26 LMGs, two 37-mm guns, four mortars, and a '75' *portee*. For transport he had some Bedford trucks, and a motley assortment of lorries commandeered locally. Also under Leclerc's command there would be the two LRDG patrols, T and G, whose task would be to act as an advance guard during the advance, and reconnoitre Uweinat, where the enemy held a garrison. The whole force would leave Faya (Leclerc's main base) on January 26. The route would be to Ounianga Kebir, which Leclerc had selected as his advance base – it lay 125 miles to the north-east – and thence via Sarra and Bishara

Free French commander: General Leclerc

Wells to Kufra.

The Free French forces at this period had many virtues but unfortunately security was not among them. For days before Leclerc marched a common greeting in the streets of Faya was 'Vers Kufra'. The Italians had already noticed the increased radio traffic in the area and were left in no doubt as to what was about to happen. All their garrisons were put on the alert and their aircraft began intensive patrolling across the desert.

The operation did not begin happily. The French trucks began to suffer from mechanical trouble, owing to the rough terrain, and on the second day a violent sand-storm blew up. This brought the French to a standstill and the LRDG patrols pushed on past stationary vehicles with the men huddled round them. Even for the desert veterans the conditions were abnormally bad, and the guardsmen found themselves weeping into their goggles. However, by evening they reached a sheltered depression with a lake in its centre, and on the far side of the lake was the fort of Ounianga Kebir.

On the morning of January 31, leaving Crichton-Stuart and G Patrol behind, Clayton and T Patrol pushed on to reconnoitre Gebel Sherif, the enemy post 60 miles south of Kufra. His force consisted of 11 cars and 44 men. Making good progress, he reached the well at Bishara, to find that it was destroyed, and as there were some fresh tracks around it, decided to move north and hide in a range of low hills. Here in a rocky valley, Clayton ordered his men to disperse and camouflage the trucks, but before long the force was spotted. Across the desert came roaring seven trucks of the Auto-Saharan Company – the enemy equivalent of the LRDG – supported by three aircraft. The Italians opened fire at once, both with machine guns and four Breda cannons, one of the finest weapons the Italian Army ever produced. Before Clayton could get his force moving, three trucks were blown up. Acting coolly, he tried to withdraw the remainder of his force to the south, intending to stage a counter-attack. But now he was attacked by the aircraft commanded by Captain Moreschini, and it was not long before he was wounded, and his truck put out of action. He had no option but to surrender.

Another truck was driven by Moore, a trooper of the New Zealand cavalry, and with him he had two guardsmen, Easton and Winchester, the former being wounded in the throat. The fourth member of the crew, an ordnance fitter called Tighe, was suffering from some internal injury. Heading away from the action, their truck was caught by the aircraft and, as the bombs began exploding, they left it and ran into the rocks for cover. From here they watched the Italians inspect the scene of action but no one came towards them; and when night came on and they were shivering in their shirts, they discussed their course of action. The alternatives – neither very pleasant – were to make the 70 mile journey to Kufra and surrender, or retrace the tracks of the patrol southwards for two or three hundred miles and hope to be picked up. Moore, the natural leader of the party, was for the second course, and after some discussion it was agreed on. Fortunately from the wreckage of the truck the men were able to salvage a two-gallon tin of water, but there was no food. The story of these four men illustrates vividly the dangers faced by the LRDG and indeed anyone operating in the desert, and is worth telling in some detail. This account is taken from the Scots Guards Regimental Orders of April 17, 1941:

Under the implicit leadership of Moore, they set out on their incredible march, carrying in turn the precious tin of water. That day, an Italian aircraft flew over them but apparently did not see them.

On the third day, they found a two-pound pot of plum jam, dropped off one of the trucks on the journey northward. They ate the whole of it that day. On the fourth day Tighe became very tired and on the fifth eventually persuaded his comrades to leave him, as he felt he was hindering their progress. Before going they poured his share of the tin water into a bottle which they had picked up.

On the sixth day a violent sand-storm arose, but Moore, Easton, and Winchester just managed to follow the fast disappearing car tracks to

Sarra. Here they spent some time in a ruined hut. They found no food, but with some motor oil which had been abandoned there they managed to bathe their feet and make a fire to warm themselves at night. They had walked 130 miles.

The next morning they continued on towards Tekro, still 160 miles distant. By now, the motor tracks had entirely disappeared over long stretches of the route, so that great difficulty was experienced in following them up. Meanwhile, Tighe, who had struggled on through all that seventh day, managed to reach the hut by nightfall, but was too exhausted to go further.

On the evening of the ninth day a French patrol, fresh from a reconnaissance of the enemy position at Kufra, found Tighe at Sarra. He was still conscious and his first thought was to explain that his three companions were ahead of him. A search party was at once organised by the French but was unsuccessful in following the tracks in the dark. The same day, two French aircraft spotted Moore and Winchester. By now, all water had given out and Easton was lagging behind. The aircraft dropped food and a bottle of lemonade – all they had with them – but the food neither Moore nor Winchester noticed and the cork came out of the lemonade bottle on impact with the ground, so that only half an inch of liquid remained. After this, the two men went on independently, Moore ahead and poor Winchester semi-delirious struggling after him. Finally, on the tenth day, another search party found first Easton about 55 miles south of Sarra and then Winchester 12 miles further on. Both could walk no more and were lying exhausted on the sand. The party came up with Moore, 70 miles south of Sarra, and 210 miles from his starting point. He was still plodding on with swinging arms. Perfectly clear-headed and normal, he waved to them without stopping as if to an acquaintance during a walking race.'

For his leadership and courage Moore was awarded the DCM and Guardsman John Easton, who died from his wound after the rescue, received a posthumous Mention in Despatches.

But to return to the patrol. With Clayton's capture, the command devolved on Captain Ballantyne, who decided that as the Italians had now brought up two armoured cars it was impossible to continue the action, and led the survivors back to rejoin G Patrol and Leclerc. At a brief conference the latter decided to make a temporary base at Tekro, send back the LRDG patrols, then make a reconnaissance in force to Kufra. It was agreed that Ballantyne and one of T Patrol trucks should go with the French as navigator. The remaining trucks were ordered back to Cairo.

Leclerc reached Kufra on February 7 and went into action that night. While a small party raided the administrative centre at Giof, de Guillebon led three trucks to the airfield and set fire to a plane there. The conflagration seemed to wake up the Italian garrison in the fort who started firing wildly into the darkness and letting off green Very lights. Unfortunately, these were the signal for the French reserves to advance and to de Guillebon's dismay, 12 Bedfords with their headlamps on came roaring up to the oasis. Soon they were stuck on

Eyes in the desert: 30-cwt truck on reconnaissance. *Below:* **A patrol loads up stores before setting out from Desert Headquarters**

he soft sand, and there was chaos while the garrison fired off a large proportion of their ammunition.

However, the reconnaissance had given Leclerc sufficient information to launch his main attack and on February 17 he moved forward from Sarra. Soon he came under attack from the Auto-Sahara companies, but swift thinking by de Guillebon out-manoeuvred them, and by evening the Italians were heading towards Tazerbo. This swung events in Leclerc's favour, for with their mobile striking force gone, the Italians shut up in the fort lost courage, and after a sustained effort from the French '75', were ready to discuss terms. On the morning of the 28th a Libyan soldier walked out of the fort under a white flag, and having been brought to Leclerc's headquarters, produced a note suggesting that the wounded of both sides should be placed in a neutral area against which no fire should be directed. To this Leclerc replied that he would only treat with an officer in person, and at 1600 hours an officer arrived. Repeating the request, he asked, 'For my purely personal information, could you tell me what the terms of surrender might be?' Realising that the enemy was almost finished, Leclerc told his patrols to increase their pressure, and ordered the officer commanding the '75' to double his rate of fire. This action had the desired effect and when dawn broke on March 1 Leclerc saw the white flag fluttering at the masthead of the fort. An hour later he drove in, to find the garrison, which consisted of 64 Italians and 352 Libyans, paraded in the courtyard. Their armament consisted of no less than 53 machine-guns and four 20-mm Bredas, and with this they could have held for weeks, given courage and the will to fight. As it was they were terrified of the French colonial troops and pleaded with Leclerc to keep them out of the fort. Mercifully, he agreed, and placed a French priest, le père Bronner, at the gate to act as sentry. To complete the comic opera atmosphere in which the operation ended was the commander's last signal, a copy of which was found in his office:
'We are in extremis. Long live Italy. Long live the King Emperor. Long live the Duce. Rome I embrace you.'

The Italians had held Kufra for 10 years and 40 days, but now their reign was ended forever. So far as the LRDG was concerned, they now had a most useful base from which operations would be conducted for many months to come.

Throughout January and well into February Wavell's triumphant advance continued across Cyrenaica. Tobruk fell, Derna, Barce, Benghazi, Agedabia, and finally El Agheila. No less than eight Italian divisions were completely destroyed, and large numbers of aircraft. In all Wavell and his two divisions took 130,000 prisoners, 850 guns and 400 tanks, apart from soft skinned vehicles. It was one of the most complete victories in military history.

But Wavell had no time to relax, for already important decisions had been reached in London: the British flank would be secured no further west than Benghazi, and support would be sent to the Greeks who were threatened by attack from the Axis powers. To complicate matters even further, there was increasing evidence that Hitler planned to take a hand in North Africa and soon there were rumours of the arrival of a force called the Afrika Korps under General Rommel. The rumours were true. On March 31, long before either side imagined he was ready for action, Rommel went into action at El Agheila, and then in a swift advance pushed Wavell's forces back to the Egyptian frontier. Rommell possessed better tanks and heavier anti-tank guns than the British and was obviously a more dangerous opponent than Graziani. He was also a general who understood the war of rapid movement; and the task of the LRDG – especially when his air strength increased – was obviously going to be much harder. Fortunately Tobruk held out and so Rommel judged it unwise to advance beyond the Egyptian frontier. Also, two other places

Above: Italian resistance crumbles: prisoners near Tobruk, 1941
Below: The new enemy: men of Rommel's Afrika Korps in action

Fast moving and brilliantly led, the Afrika Korps seizes the initiative

remained in British hands – Kufra, and Jarabub, the latter being to the north of the Great Sand Sea, and about 150 miles south of Sollum. From Jarabub and Siwa, 100 miles further east, the LRDG operated a squadron, while the remainder of the Group remained in Kufra, where Colonel Bagnold became Garrison Commander.

The summer of 1941 was a frustrating one for the LRDG. A good deal of energy was taken up with keeping Kufra supplied, for the Sudan Defence Force, who were responsible for the task, had little idea of what they were up against. It was not until July that they took over the place and Bagnold's patrols were free to roam again. There were other problems. Guy Prendergast, who had at last arrived as second-in-command, saw at once that the Group must have its own aircraft to operate efficiently, and began pestering the RAF. The junior service, however, determined to keep everything that flew under its own control, proved stubborn, and

Left and below: **Road watch: from a concealed position men of the LRDG keep an eye on enemy troop movements**

eventually Prendergast had to persuade the army to buy two light WACO machines from their Egyptian owners. In August Prendergast took over from Bagnold, who was promoted to Brigadier and became Deputy Signals Officer-in-Chief Middle East.

Though frustrated, the LRDG was not inactive at this period. T Patrol reconnoitred the Sirte Desert, the area inland from El Agheila; other patrols carried out road watches; and officers were sent off to run courses on navigation – the army had begun to realise that, unlike LRDG patrols, too many units got lost once they left the coast road. Mitford took a patrol beyond the Kalansho Sand Sea to reconnoitre the Jalo area, and there were many minor operations of this kind, useful if not dramatic or spectacular. By the time the summer was over, the unit was looking forward to playing an active rôle in the coming offensive. But, in fact, had it known, an interview had already taken place in Cairo which was to have a great impact on its operational rôle, and involve it in some of the most extraordinary episodes of the desert war.

The subaltern from Scotland

Lt-Colonel David Stirling: he conceived and founded the Special Air Service

One morning in July 1941 a very tall, dark haired young man with a charming smile and patrician manners hobbled on crutches to the entrance of Middle East Headquarters, Cairo. Lacking a pass, he bluffed his way past the sentries, lurched down a corridor and entered the office of a major on the Adjutant-General's staff. Apologising for his unceremonious arrival, the subaltern said that his name was David Stirling, his regiment was the Scots Guards, and he was serving with No. 8 Commando. He had important business with the Commander-in-Chief, General Auchinleck, who had recently taken over from Wavell. Unimpressed, and having formed a hostile attitude towards Stirling whilst instructing on a tactical course – the latter's party-going habits rendered him somewhat dozy in the mornings – the major refused to help him, or even to listen to his ideas. Then the telephone rang; it was a report from the gate that an officer had entered the headquarters without a pass. While the major took the call, Stirling slipped out of his office, took a few awkward paces down the corridor, and entered a door marked DCGS. The initials meant nothing to him, but the man seated at the desk was very familiar. He was General Neil Ritchie, Deputy Chief-of-Staff, Middle East Forces. Now in the British Army, for a subaltern to enter the office of a general without an appointment is unusual; to enter uninvited is quite unheard of. If Stirling had been anything but an extraordinary character, he would have mumbled his apologies and fled. But being the man he was, he stood his ground, apologized for the unconventional manner of his arrival and insisted that he had vital matters of operational importance to bring before the general. For a moment there was an awkward pause, and then perhaps because of the bond between Scot and Scot, or perhaps because he recognized Stirling's unusual air of authority, Ritchie asked him to be seated. So the conversation began. Pulling out a memorandum and reading from it rapidly, Stirling explained that he wanted to destroy Rommel's air force on the ground. His method would be to form a small unit of picked men and parachute behind the enemy lines before the next offensive. Ritchie took the document, read it carefully, then looked up and said that it might well be the sort of plan the GOC was looking for. Once it had been studied in detail, Stirling would be called for a further discussion. With this he summoned the DAAG who, concealing his surprise, found himself landed with the administrative arrangements, should the plan go ahead. Out in the corridor he warned Stirling that he would do his duty, but nothing more.

In the British Army families and family connections count for a good deal, perhaps for too much. Making enquiries, Ritchie was reassured to find that Stirling came from good stock and his ancestors had fought on the borders for centuries; moreover he had two brothers in the Scots Guards and another was third secretary in the British Embassy in Cairo. He may also have been interested to learn that before the war, David had been training himself to become the first man to conquer Mount Everest. His injuries, incidentally, were due to a parachute jumping accident; the silk was ripped on the tail unit of the plane, with the result that he came down far too fast and injured his back and legs. He was now recovering, but the period of enforced idleness in hospital had given him time to think; and the more he pondered the organisation of No 8 Commando, the more convinced he became that it was too large and too immobile. What was needed was a much smaller unit which could travel fast, do its job in an hour or so and get away again. If a raid succeeded, then the loss to the enemy would be great; if it failed, then the loss to the unit would be minimal. As an example of the economic use of manpower, Stirling reasoned, his idea could hardly be bettered.

The reasoning was not lost on Auchinleck, now under pressure from Churchill to launch his army into action before it was ready. So three days after his interview with Ritchie, Stirling found himself back at GHQ and being given permission to go ahead. He could recruit six officers and 60 men and set up a training camp in the Suez Canal Zone. His unit would come under the direct command of the

**General Neil Ritchie, right, the man
who had faith in Stirling, talks
with General Sir Claude Auchinleck**

GOC and its first task would be to raid
advanced German airfields the night
before the November offensive. Stirling himself would be promoted to the
rank of captain and his command
would be known as L Detachment of
the SAS Brigade. These initials meant
Special Air Service and were applied
to a unit which did not exist, the idea
being to trick the enemy into believing that parachute troops had arrived
in the Middle East. These details were
explained by Auchinleck in person
who, as the interview closed, shook
hands with Stirling and wished him
good luck. Stirling was now handed
over to the Director of Military
Intelligence, and then the A and Q
Staff (who deal with administration
and supplies) to fix the details of raising and operating his unit. Not surprisingly the atmosphere was somewhat reserved, if not hostile.

To anyone who has served in the
army (and not only the British Army)
the reason for this will be obvious. As
a race, professional soldiers detest
special forces, or 'Private armies' as
they are often called. This is partly

jealousy of the publicity and chances
for promotion that such units create,
and partly a rooted belief that they
absorb more men and supplies than
their results warrant. Orthodox military opinion is that a good standard
unit can be trained to do anything.
No doubt aware of this attitude,
Stirling was hardly surprised when Q
Branch told him that no tents were
available and he would have to wait
his turn. It was obvious, too, that he
would have to fight for other supplies,
from dixies and cooking equipment
upwards. However, the saving factor
was that his unit came directly under
the GOC and in time his supplies must
be found somewhere – or Auchinleck
would want to know why. So for the
moment Stirling concentrated on
recruiting.

As might be expected, there was no
shortage of volunteers. For officers he
chose Jock Lewes, a daring soldier but
also a fine scholar and organiser; an
Irishman called McGonigal; two
Englishmen called Bonnington and
Thomas; and a Scot called Bill Fraser,

---

1 Few more striking manifestations of this
attitude are available than the vitriolic treatment of Major-General Orde Wingate in volume
3 of the British official war history, *The war
against Japan.*

Stirling, right, with Paddy Mayne

The Wylies Jeep
used by the SAS in the western desert, it was less capacious than the 30-cwt
Chevrolet but more easy to conceal. It was armed with one .5-inch Browning
machine gun, and two pairs of Vickers K aircraft machine guns

The British .303 Vickers Machine-gun
This reliable and accurate weapon was the standard medium machine gun
throughout the war years in the British Army. In its vehicle mounted role it was used
extensively in the desert raids. *Action:* Recoil with gas boost. *Coolant:* water.
Weight: 40 lbs with water. *Ammunition:* .303 ball in canvas belts.
Rate of fire: 450-550 rounds-per-minute

whose father and grandfather had been NCOs in the Gordon Highlanders. Finally, he recruited Paddy Mayne, an Irish international rugby player of enormous physique – actually he was under close arrest at this time for knocking out a superior officer – who when convinced that there was a real chance of hitting the enemy agreed to serve. Under what terms he was released from arrest it is not clear, but by the following day he was with Stirling and at work.

Camp was set up at Kabrit, a village on the edge of the Great Bitter Lake. All it consisted of was three tents – two small ones for the men and a large one for stores – a notice bearing the unit's name – and a few tables, benches and chairs. Except that it was smaller, it looked like any other camp in the Canal Zone, and the heat, the dust, the flies, and the bare, featureless landscape were common to all.

But Stirling did not intend to continue existing on this level of subsistence, and had already reconnoitred a lavish camp belonging to the New Zealanders a few miles away, which happened to be empty, guarded by a few Indian sentries. The night raid – his unit's first operation – was a great success, and yielded not only 15 small tents, but large quantities of furniture and equipment, including a piano. Within 24 hours Stirling had the smartest little camp for miles around.

The next job was training. From the start Stirling made it clear that, despite the unit's irregular role, there would be nothing slapdash about turn-out, performance on parade, or general behaviour. When the men went on leave into Cairo there would be no boasting or bragging; all toughness would be reserved for action against the enemy. A good deal of the training was routine: PT, map reading, shooting, and stripping down weapons, including Italian Barettas and German Schmeissers, but Stirling also laid on night exercises in the desert. By every means at his disposal he tried to improve his men's physical endurance and quicken their reaction. Men who panicked in emergency were no use to him. Then came the parachute training, rather sketchy and improvised, and two men were killed when their parachutes failed to open.

However, as often happens, such a mishap gave Stirling a chance to demonstrate his own courage and the following day he was the first to jump.

From early November onwards, preparations for the first operations increasingly occupied his attention. The plan, an ambitious one, was to raid five forward aerodromes simultaneously, and so deal with the bulk of Rommel's fighter force. There were great problems though, not the least concerning the explosives to be used. How could a small party carry sufficient explosives and incendiary bombs to destroy all the aircraft and their engines? After long discussion it was agreed that the only answer was a bomb combining both functions, but an expert who came down from Cairo was not optimistic. Tests would take months, even years, he warned, to Stirling's fury. With his departure it was obvious that if the unit wanted a special bomb it would have to invent it on the spot, and Jock Lewes began experiments. After two noisy weeks and many failures, he succeeded in preparing an explosive incendiary bomb weighing just under a pound, but powerful enough to deal with an aircraft. Estimating that a man could carry two dozen bombs, the destructive power of the unit was therefore enormous – assuming, of course, that it could get at the aircraft.

Opinion in Cairo – except that of Auchinleck and Ritchie – was that it could not. During this training period staff officers both from the army and the RAF came down to Kabrit and expressed themselves astonished at what was going on. How Stirling had sold his crazy idea, they could not imagine . . . obviously his powers of persuasion, they usually added, must be greater than his military knowledge.

But Stirling was undeterred. In fact, the persecution from GHQ sharpened his resolve, and after some barbed comments from a Group Captain of the RAF he took on a bet that his unit could raid Heliopolis airfield and stick labels on the planes instead of bombs. The operation was planned with great care, 40 men taking part; they got on to the airfield without trouble, stuck on 45 labels, and slipped out again unseen. Somewhat astonished, the Group Captain sent Stirling a cheque for ten pounds and a letter stating that airfield defences would be improved. Rumour had it that 'rockets' were flying in all directions for some time and the security officers at Heliopolis were walking around somewhat shaken. What mattered to Stirling was that he had proved his point.

But now it was time to move from war games to war. Auchinleck's offensive aimed at pushing Rommel out of Cyrenaica and relieving Tobruk was to begin at dawn on November 18, 1941. The previous night, so it was planned, the SAS would attack five airfields in the Gazala-Tmimi area, the men being parachuted down in the darkness, some twenty-four hours in advance. During daylight on the 17th they would hide up in the rocky escarpment running south from the coast road and take observations of

Right: Time for a break: three beards – two cigarettes
Below: Deep in the enemy territory, survival demands that at least one man is on look-out

their targets. At night they would make for the airfields, cut their way through the wire and place their bombs, then set off for a rendezvous with 'A' Squadron LRDG who would carry them back to the base at Siwa.

Though it might seem simple, the operation needed a great deal of planning, and caused a number of problems. It was the first parachute operation in the Desert campaign and the job of packing bombs, fuses, guns, and ammunition, ready for the drop, was only completed after a good deal of chopping and changing.

Then the weather deteriorated. On the morning of the 16th a wind sprang up and the forecasts were that rain would come during the next forty-eight hours. By 1700 hours the wind had increased to gale force, and chances of mounting the operation at all seemed pretty slim. Instead of landing in a group, Stirling's men would probably come down all over the desert, many of them injured, and unable to find their equipment. The Brigadier General Staff at GHQ, who was responsible to Auchinleck for the operation, advised Stirling to cancel

In spite of its age (it was obsolete in 1939) the Bristol Bombay Bomber-Transport did sterling service in the Middle East theatre. *Engines:* **Two 1,010 hp Bristol Pegasus XXII radials.** *Span:* **95 feet 9 inches.** *Max speed:* **192 mph**

it, but left the final decision to him. Stirling's reaction was to drive to 216 Squadron RAF where his officers were waiting near the transport planes and discuss the situation. His position was a most unenviable one. If he cancelled, there would be laughter among the wags at GHQ, coupled with insinuations that SAS was more fit for comic opera than war. If, on the other hand, he let things go ahead and then failed, accusations would start flying that he was incompetent and his ideas not worth fourpence. However, Stirling was more concerned with his men's morale than with chatter in Cairo; he knew that, if the operation were cancelled for any reason whatsoever, their confidence would be shaken. Jock Lewes's reaction was that in war conditions were never perfect, and if the unit waited for ideal conditions, they would wait forever. The other officers were in agreement. So with relief Stirling signalled the BGS that the raid would go ahead as planned.

At 1915 hours the five Bombay transports warmed up their engines and the SAS went aboard. Apart from Stirling himself, Mayne, Lewes, McGonigal, were in charge of planes, Fraser and Thomas serving as second-in-command. The ride was not a comfortable one, the men sprawled out on the floor and their equipment stacked towards the tail. Few people talked; and some tried to sleep, though without much success. Bomber Command had arranged to drop flares over the

coastline to assist the Bombays in charting their course, but the storm had raised so much sand that nothing could be seen. To complicate matters the planes had to swerve off course to avoid ack-ack fire and Stirling began to wonder if the whole expedition would not end up in losing itself.

Then a warning came from the flight-sergeant: they would be over the dropping zone in six minutes. Quickly the doors were opened and the rush of cold air brought everyone to the alert. Slowly the minutes ticked by . . . four minutes to go . . . two minutes . . . one minute . . . Then the green light flashed and Stirling moved forward a few paces then jumped. In quick succession the men followed; there was no hestiation. Outside the plane it was pitch dark and impossible to tell when the impact of hitting the ground would come. To Stirling it came without warning, as a crushing blow which knocked him unconscious. Coming to, he found himself being dragged along the ground and instinctively released himself before rolling on his back. Gradually testing out his limbs, he found that nothing was broken, so got to his feet and began flashing his torch. For some while there was no response, and in fact it took an hour to assemble the men – except one who could not be found at all, – and learn that they were all hurt or gashed to some degree. Almost as bad, only two out of ten supply cannisters could be found; and these contained blankets,

water bottles, food, and half a dozen tins of Lewes bombs, but without fuses. So far as blowing up planes was concerned, the unit was powerless. Stirling had made his first mistake.

Nevertheless it was no use staying where they were, Stirling decided to send the unit to the rendezvous, while he and Sergeant Tait went north towards the coast road. If he could not destroy aircraft, he could at least carry out a reconnaissance. Theoretically it should have been only ten miles away, but, as it soon became clear, the party had been dropped too far south, and not until 0430 hrs. did they reach the escarpment. At 0530 hrs. it began to rain, a most extraordinary sight in this area, and soon the *wadis* had become great torrents. Time and again the two men found themselves wading up to their thighs, their only comfort being that they would not go thirsty and could not be spotted by enemy aircraft. But the weather grew so bad that even a limited reconnaissance was obviously impossible, and reluctantly Stirling turned south for the rendezvous. Reaching it he saw Jake Easonsmith of the LRDG brewing up over a fire, then Fraser and Jock Lewes. Their experience had been roughly the same as his and they had accomplished nothing. When Paddy Mayne turned up his story was just as pitiful; and of McGonigal's and Bonnington's parties there was no sign whatever. After another day and a half of waiting, Stirling decided that he must head

back for Siwa; of seven officers and 55 men who had started on the operation, only four officers and 18 men were left. Instead of proving his case to GHQ, he had landed himself with a fiasco.

But if depressed he was not despairing, for this operation, abortive as it turned out, had taught him a good deal. To begin with he had moved freely on the enemy flank. Secondly, he had seen how the LRDG operated. They had carried the survivors including himself 250 miles over the desert to Siwa without any problem at all; and if they could take him back from a raid, he reasoned, they could take him to it. Ruefully he had to admit that the hazards of a parachute drop rendered this method of delivery quite impractical. But would the LRDG co-operate? Could they fit his operations into an already crowded schedule? His conversations with Jake Easonsmith, and later contacts with Don Steele left no doubt. As Kennedy Shaw has recorded: 'It was an ideal partnership. We could exploit to the full what was our greatest asset – the ability to deliver a passenger anywhere behind the enemy's lines at any time asked.' And weeks of training had made the SAS fine artists into getting into – and out of – places at night.

However, granted LRDG co-operation, there were still organizational problems. To begin with Stirling knew that he could not call on Auchinleck for reinforcements – the GOC and his staff had enough on their plates with the offensive – and would have to use the officers and men that were left. Secondly, he would have to bring his base forward from Kubrit.

Flying back to Cairo, Stirling found a big flap going on. Suddenly halting his retreat, Rommel had reorganised, then swiftly moved his army round the Allied flank. Finding Cunningham unable to cope with the situation, Auchinleck had sent forward Ritchie to take over the 8th Army, and soon it was advancing again. A few days later Stirling had a brief interview with the latter at his forward headquarters, and was relieved to find that, despite its initial failure there was no intention of

winding up his unit. Equally, there was no time to give detailed orders, and he was being more or less left to fashion his own role. This suited him admirably.

So the next few weeks saw Stirling and his diminutive unit settling in at Jalo, an oasis near the north-west corner of the Kalansho Sand Sea. It was, of course, a long way behind the front, but its distance from the coastal strip where the main action was taking place, rendered it fairly secure. (If one imagines an inverted isoseles triangle with sides some 200 miles long, Benghazi is top left, Tobruk top right, and Jalo at the bottom.) Jalo had little to recommend it so far as scenery or amenities were concerned; the water from the oasis was salty, mud huts clustered round the fort, and even the palm trees survived with some difficulty. The place had been taken on November 24 by a flying column composed of the 2nd Punjab and the 6th South African Armoured Car Regiment, under Brigadier D W Reid. Though food and petrol were short, Reid welcomed Stirling and SAS, and put them on the ration strength. Happily Don Steele and 'A' Squadron of the LRDG had moved to Jalo also and planning could begin at once on new operations. The situation was as favourable now as it would ever be.

Left: Italian LMG post: a thorn bush is better than no cover at all
Below: It can be cold in the desert: men of the New Zealand Patrol LRDG prepare to move out

The raids from Jalo

During December 1941 Rommel continued to retreat, his plan being to get back to Agedabia and El Agheila, so handing to the British the problems of a lengthy line of communications. Though somewhat mauled, his forces were still intact and full of fight; and at any moment it was possible that he might regroup and deliver yet another of his lightning armoured thrusts. In early December Reid informed Stirling that he had orders to move north-west from Jalo and make contact with Brigadier J C O Marriott and the 22nd Guards Brigade. The move was part of a major plan to trap Rommel as he retreated towards Benghazi. Unfortunately Reid was being held up by shortage of petrol and supplies, and it did not look as if he could leave till about December 22. Even then, he was worried about being caught from the air on the last 20 miles of the journey – his column had been harassed by both Italian and German fighters en route for Jalo – and wondered if

Stirling could raid Agedabia airfield a few hours before his advance – on the night of the 21st/22nd. Stirling agreed, but in the days that followed – anxious because at any moment he expected a signal to return to Cairo – worked on detailed plans for enlarging the operation. With Paddy Mayne and ten men he would raid Sirte airfield, which lay far to the west, some 170 miles beyond El Agheila and therefore 350 from Jalo; two days later Jock Lewes would set out for El Agheila; and eight days after that, on the 21st, Bill Fraser would lead the raid against Agedabia, as requested by Brigadier Reid. Given success on these three airfields – Sirte was said to be one of Rommel's largest airfields – the German air strength should be hit a damaging blow.

It was on December 8 that Stirling and his party left Jalo. Transporting them was Gus Holliman and the Rhodesian patrol. Holliman, who had formerly served in the Royal Tank Corps, had been with LRDG for a year, had carried out some long desert journeys and ferried petrol on the 400-mile haul from Wadi Halfa to Gilf Kebir, for the operations south of Kufra. As Stirling could see at once, he knew exactly what he was up to. The column, which totalled 32 officers and men, travelled in seven 30-cwt trucks, piled high with stores and equipment, petrol, food, and water, with the men riding uncomfortably wherever they could find room. In the first truck rode Michael Sadler, the Rhodesian navigator, alongside Holliman, and Stirling followed in the second. The first day the journey was without major incident and just before dark the trucks lagered for the night. Tuning in to Prendergast's headquarters, the radio operator learned that the opposing armies to the north-west were static; Rommel was at Gazala and the 8th Army was re-organising for its next advance. The journey continued over the desert for two more days and except for some mechanical trouble in one of the trucks, nothing much happened. All round the desert lay calm and empty and there was not even the sight of wandering Arabs. On the 11th, however when the column was some 60 miles to the south of Sirte, things began to

Final check before leaving

change. By now the ground had become rocky and the going was harder; at noon Holliman decided to look for cover and halt, both for lunch and to give Sadler time to check their position. At this precise moment an Italian Ghiblis flew out of the desert and dropped its bombs, apparently untouched by the curtain of fire from the Lewis guns.

Reacting swiftly, Holliman gave orders that the column must race to a patch of scrub a few miles back and attempt to hide there. In fact, the scrub was barely two feet high, but when the trucks were in position and the scrim nets stretched across, visibility was reduced to some extent. The Ghiblis was a scout aircraft equipped with radio, and, as the LRDG knew to their cost, unless it could be shot down before getting a signal back to base, it was not long before the bombers arrived.

When they came there were three of them, and for a quarter of an hour they strafed the scrub with machine-guns then dropped stick after stick of bombs. From the noise and the dust that was flying, it seemed that the raiders must have suffered heavy casualties, but when the aircraft flew away again, Stirling was relieved to find that no one was wounded, and the trucks had suffered no damage whatsoever.

Two hours later Holliman decided it was time to move on, and the column headed over flat country broken by salt marshes and low sand dunes. By 1630 hours Sadler reckoned they were about 40 miles from Sirte; and Holliman decided that as it would be dark in an hour he would go on to a ridge about three miles from the coastal road. Here Stirling and his men could lie up and observe their target, and the LRDG party could head south again

A word before leaving: David Stirling gives final orders to patrol commander, Lieutenant Edward McDonald

The German 7.92-mm MG-42:
A dual purpose light or heavy machine gun. *Action:* recoil. *Coolant:* air.
Weight: 26.5 lbs or 42.3 lbs with tripod. *Length:* 48 in. *Ammunition:* 7.92-mm ball in belts of metal links. *Rate of fire:* 800-900 rounds-per-minute

into the desert. But no sooner as the decision was taken than a second Ghiblis appeared and began circling the column. Holliman's opinion was that the hour was too late for it to call up the bombers, but it would report their presence. What the Italians would imagine was going on, it was impossible to say; but undoubtedly they would be on the alert.

When darkness fell the column was still 20 miles from the road and had to go without lights as best it could. At nine o'clock, when it was clear that their destination could not be far away, there was a signal from the rear truck and Holliman ordered all engines to be switched off. Listening intently, Stirling could hear excited voices shouting and then cars starting up and roaring away into the distance. No doubt, he thought, a patrol had been sent out, following the signal from the Ghiblis, and now all chance of surprise was lost.

What was to be done? Stirling could not face the consequence of another fiasco and yet was loathe to turn back with nothing accomplished. A few moments thought and his mind was made up. Paddy Mayne must take ten men a further 30 miles along the coast to the airfield at Tamet; and he himself and a Sergeant Brough would see what could be done at Sirte. Quickly Holliman was told the plan and he agreed; three trucks would pick up each party, then drive to a rendezvous 80 miles south in the desert. Both raids would take place at 2300 hours the following night so that one would not give the alarm before the other could be completed.

Making as much noise as he could, Holliman revved up his engines then led the column away from the road and into the desert. Stirling and Brough headed north for the airfield which they calculated was about three miles away. In the darkness they came across it suddenly, before encountering any sentries or barbed wire, and across their front stretched long rows of aircraft. Resisting the temptation to put his bombs on them without delay, Stirling decided to

When stationary – concealment. A crew drag camouflage nets into position

carry out a thorough reconnaissance. Unfortunately two soldiers were sleeping on the perimeter of the field, and when Stirling and Brough stumbled on them in the darkness they let out loud cries, and soon sentries were firing in all directions. Then some gunners began firing out to sea, obviously convinced that the threat from inland must be a diversion preluding a commando raid.

Amused rather than apprehensive, Stirling and Brough headed for the ridge marked on the map and soon were able to conceal themselves among the scrub. Here they slept soundly and it was bright daylight before they awoke, to find that they had a fine view of the airfield and about 30 Caprioni bombers. During the morning aircraft took off and landed, but afternoon brought a most unwelcome development; two by two the bombers took off, and by five o'clock the place was empty. All Stirling could do was curse his fate, and hope that Paddy Mayne would have better luck. There were still some six hours to wait and in the darkness the two men made their way down to the road which they reached soon after 2200 hours. There was no traffic and the night was calm and peaceful. It was eleven . . . eleven-thirty . . . midnight . . . and still not a sound came from the direction of Tamet. The future existence of his unit, Stirling reflected, must now be hanging on a thread. Then came a great flash to the west followed by the sound of bombs going off, one after the other. It was the sweetest sound Stirling had heard in a whole lifetime. Happily he waited for Holliman and the trucks which appeared dead on time at 0045 hours. Before heading for the rendezvous with Paddy Mayne, Stirling stayed on a few minutes to mine the road, and was delighted to watch an Italian truck get blown up. By this time, of course, he was already heading south across the desert.

It was 1100 hours next morning before Mayne and his party reached the rendezvous, but they had good news to bring. Having got on to the airfield at Tamet they felt their way to a group of buildings. Inside one of these they could hear people chatting and laughing – it was probably the officers' mess. Flinging open the door, Paddy

sprayed the room with his Tommy gun then got away fast, while four of his men acted as a rear-guard. Sprinting with five men across the field, he now reached the aircraft and began putting on bombs – 23 of them. The twenty-fourth aircraft had to be immobilised by ripping out the instrument panel. Now it was time to run, but the party had barely gone 50 yards before the planes started going up. In the distance they could see lights being flashed apparently from the LRDG and according to the agreed signal. But, as it soon transpired, the Italians were flashing as well, so before they knew what had happened, Paddy and his men were off course. The only hope now was to blow some blasts on a whistle and hope these would be answered. Mercifully the LRDG were not far away and the plan worked. Leaping into the trucks the raiders were soon roaring away from the blazing aircraft and towards the relative safety of the sands.

Back at Jalo Stirling had to wait several days before his other parties returned. Jock Lewes had been completely unlucky at El Agheila, which so it appeared was only a ferrying point. But when Bill Fraser got back from Agedabia he could boast the greatest prize of all: 37 aircraft destroyed on the ground. On the return journey they had met Brigadier Reid and his Oasis Force, which was camping for the night in the Wadi el Faregh. Later Reid wrote in his diary 'At first light there was a certain amount of excitement among the forward troops . . . I drove forward to see what was the matter and met Fraser of Stirling's L Detachment whom I eagerly asked how he had got on. He said, 'Very sorry, sir; I had to leave two aircraft on the ground as I ran out of explosives; but we destroyed 37. This indeed was a wonderful achievement by one officer and three men. Incidentally, we heard later that Rommel had been in Agedabia that night. He must have had a bit of a headache.'

In contrast to this enthusiasm from an officer on the spot, it is interesting

The man and the weapon: Corporal John Henderson on guard with Medium Machine-gun

'. . . the most arid place on earth . . .'

to note the cautious attitude of the Official War historians. In the British history, 'The Mediterranean and the Middle East', Volume III, Stirling's achievements at Tamet and Agedabia are referred to merely as 'claims'. And Signor Manzetti in the Italian Official History, 'Seconda Offensiva Brittanica in Africa Settentrionale' gives the figures as 11 aircraft lost at Tamet and 'about 15' at Agedabia. Even at this reduced total the raids would have been a great success; but there is no reason to doubt Mayne's and Fraser's claims. And certainly Reid and his Oasis Force was able to link up with the 22nd Guards Brigade free from air attack.

An old adage in the British Army is 'always reinforce success' and this Stirling intended to do at once. By Christmas Eve he and Paddy Mayne were back in Holliman's trucks and heading back for Sirte and Tamet – his belief being that the enemy would not expect such a swift return. As a precaution, however, the column was taking a route further to the west, Mayne and his party being dropped off at Tamet and then Stirling at Sirte. As before the navigator was Michael Sadler, who was rapidly gaining a reputation as the best man at his job in the entire LRDG. Though working with inaccurate maps, he almost invariably took his column to

where it wanted to be, and Stirling and his men were very impressed with him. On this occasion the dropping-off point was to be the Wadi Tamet, a deep ravine running north to south. From the map it seemed to offer Mayne and his men a good covered approach to the airfield. Unlike the previous journey, this one was free from air attack and soon after 2100 hours on the third day the column reached a point five miles from Tamet. Here Paddy Mayne and his party were dropped, and Holliman now proposed to hit the coastal road and drive boldly down it to Sirte so that Stirling could carry out his raid. But when they reached the road, a German armoured division was moving along it, no doubt heading for El Agheila where, so it was reported on the wireless set, Rommel was digging in. What was to be done? Convinced that the going between Tamet and Sirte was too rough across country, Holliman said they would have to wait, but four hours later, at 0230 hours the column was still moving past. It was at this time that there was a flash in the sky towards Tamet and then a rapid series of explosions. Obviously Paddy Mayne had brought off another success.

At 0300 hours the German column began to straggle and then came to an end. So climbing into their trucks, the mixed force of SAS and LRDG began moving down the road, passing enemy trucks and vehicles of all kinds bivouacked by the roadside. At any moment Stirling expected to be halted by a sentry, but nothing happened and by 0400 hours they were at a point only two miles from Sirte airfield. Though there were armoured units camping not far away on either side, Holliman decided that this should be the rendezvous, and after fixing a password, Stirling and his five men moved off towards the perimeter. With a bare hour of darkness left, they were pushed for time, and it was decided to move straight down the road. But this course proved useless, too, for soon a barricade loomed up and sentries began challenging. Reluctantly Stirling decided to return to the rendezvous; but he was still determined to do some damage, and suggested to Holliman that the column should drive down the road, shooting up anything in sight. Though such a role was outside the scope of the LRDG Holliman agreed, and the trucks were turned and lined up on the road with their bonnets pointing west towards Tamet. By now there was a faint streak of light in the horizon and delay would be fatal, so off they went. Roaring along at speed they shot up tented camps, lorries, more tents, crews who could be seen running towards their blazing vehicles, a tank carrier, two more tents. As the light and therefore the danger increased, Holliman called the cease fire and the trucks headed away from the road. Luckily, no enemy vehicles came in pursuit and before long the desert lay silent about them.

When Paddy Mayne reached the rendezvous he once more had good news. Getting on to the airfield at Tamet without trouble, he had found 27 aircraft belonging to a squadron just arrived from Italy, and had put a bomb on each one of them. Unfortunately his fuses, set at half an hour, had burned through in two-thirds of that time and the party had only just got away from their target before the first explosion came. Not unexpectedly, Stirling was treated to some friendly ribbing after his second failure, and agreed to pull himself together. But with a total of 88 enemy aircraft destroyed by his unit, he was not particularly depressed.

While the Tamet and Sirte raids were in progress Jock Lewes and Bill Fraser were on raids against Nifolia and Marble Arch, 40 and 70 miles respectively to the west of El Agheila. It was some days after his return to Jalo before Stirling received any news of them and when it came this was bad. The bearer was Lieutenant C S Morris MC of the LRDG who said that he had picked up Jock Lewes' party after the Nofilia raid and they had headed east to recover Bill Fraser's party. On the journey they were heavily attacked from the air, and five trucks had been destroyed, Lewes himself being killed. In the sole remaining truck Morris had continued to the rendezvous near Marble Arch, but Bill Fraser did not show up and there was no indication of what might have happened to him.

From Sergeant Lilley, Stirling was able to learn how Jock Lewes' raid had gone wrong. Only a few aircraft were resting on the airstrip and these were widely dispersed. Having planted a bomb on the first one, they moved to the second and had just dealt with that when the first bomb went off. Immediately the place became alive with troops and the raiding party was only just able to extricate itself. Then the column had been caught by an enemy bomber in the open desert. Later, after Jock Lewes had been hit, two fighters joined in and destroyed the trucks, the attack going on for some hours. Luckily no one else was hit, and by a process of cannibalisation one truck was got running. Slowly it was driven towards the rendezvous with Bill Fraser.

It was some days before the story of this party was learned, but it proved to be a great one and has now taken its place as an epic of courage and endurance.

Fraser had four men with him, Sergeant DuVivier and Sergeant Tait, and two private soldiers, Byrne and Phillips. Finding the airfield at Marble Arch deserted, they had returned next day to the rendezvous marked on their maps. No trucks arrived and they waited there for six days before deciding that they must try to walk back to their own lines. By now there was half a pint of water left for each man, and food for two days, and their plan was to head for Hasselet, a British position some 200 miles away. So they set off and Sergeant DuVivier recorded their experiences in his diary:

'We walked all day but found no water. Thirsty as I was I decided not to drink my remaining half-pint as it helped my morale just to hear it in the bottle. Sometimes I took a sip to moisten my mouth, but as it got less I spat it back again. Then I started to suck a couple of pebbles to keep the saliva from drying up.'

That night they lay down, each man wrapping himself in the single blanket he was carrying; and next morning after painfully swallowing a little food, set off again, hoping for better luck.

'But alas, the day went by and still no water. Then we spotted what looked like an inland lake some six miles or so to the south-east and with renewed hope we hurried our pace. We reached the water about mid-day but to our dismay found that it was salt water, so strong that it was impossible to swallow the smallest amount.'

In desperation they lit a fire and tried to distill it, but eventually found that they were using more

'the bare rock forces itself up . . . '
Africa Korps sentry on the look-out for desert raiders

water in perspiration than the job was worth. Then –

'Bob Tait suggested that two of us should carry on with the distilling while the other three made for the road and tried to raid a truck for water and provisions. We drew lots. Lieutenant Fraser and I remained and Bob, Phillips, and Byrne did the raiding.'

We could not believe our luck when they returned soon after midnight with two jerry-cans filled with crystal clear and cool water which they had got by shooting up a German truck. What a feast we had that night! We made a brew of tea and feasted on bully stew, cheese and biscuits and dried dates for dessert. That night we slept well and did not wake up before midday.'

For the next three days the men walked on till they reached the Wadi Faregh. On both sides of this enemy trucks were bivouacked, and spotting one which was somewhat isolated from the rest, the party waited till dark then marched towards it on a compass bearing. Coming up close they made a plan then went into action:

'At a given signal Lieutenant Fraser made for the driver's cabin and Byrne and I, armed with Smith and Wesson revolvers, covered Bob and Phillips whilst they 'downed' the flap and

upped' the canvas. In a matter of seconds we had grabbed the 'bodies' and pulled them out, a struggling mass in the sand. They did not put up a fight but screamed for mercy. Obviously they thought we were a gang of Arab cut-throats and we had some trouble in quietening them down.'

There was no water on the truck, but some food and a small benzine stove which it was thought would come in handy. Bluffing the Italians into believing that they were surrounded by a large British force, the party moved east, judging their position to be between El Agheila and Mersa-Brega. Desperate with thirst, they were all weak and tired and now decided that if they were to finish the journey, it must be by truck. Luckily a small Mercedes-Benz came slowly along the track towards them with two Germans. Disarming these, and putting a revolver into the driver's neck, the party set off for Mersa-Brega. The place was humming with activity but the party drove through without incident. But now things went wrong: missing the track they had used on a previous occasion, the party got bogged down in a salt marsh and had to abandon the car and let their prisoners go free. Still only 40 miles were left to the nearest British post and this was covered without difficulty in two days.

While Frazer and his party were on their journey back, yet another desert journey was in progress. When the Stukas attacked Morris's column (*en route* to the rendezvous with Fraser), a party of ten soldiers of the LRDG led by Gunner Stutterd, a New Zealander, found themselves alone in the desert with three gallons of water, nine biscuits, and a tin of emergency chocolate ration. Setting off due east, the party was attacked by two Stukas, but hid in scrub and escaped unhit. One of the men, a parachutist called White, decided to head south for Marada and try to get hold of a truck – his feet were raw with marching. So the nine pushed on through the night and the next day, walking 45 minutes then resting for 15. The water ration was now down to under half a pint per day, but the men were lucky to spot an Arab campfire in the darkness. Giving them dates and a small quantity of water, the Arabs explained that there was a spring a few miles off and offered to show them the way. When they had filled their can with water, it proved too heavy to carry in their weakened condition, and they had to drink some to bring the weight down. The following night they boiled some of the remaining water and made a chocolate drink from the emergency ration. This seemed to give them more energy and that night they covered a distance of 40 miles. Then a dust storm blew up and they had to shelter in a hole dug into the sand. It was bitterly cold in the wind and that night they suffered considerably; and though they went on next morning it was slowly and in pain, their feet becoming raw. Then they found the Italian track from Agedabia to Jalo and turned south along it. Next morning the wind had dropped and the sun was hot, so that having frozen for two days they were now being baked, but about 1100 hours Stutterd thought he could see a group of palm trees in the distance. At first a mirage was suspected but the trees became so distinct that he mentioned them to the others – and they could all see them. It was the oasis at Aujila. Using their last reserves of energy, the men set off on the five mile journey towards it, walking for short spells then collapsing in the sand to rest. By dusk they made it; found water to drink, and dug up some onions and turnips from an Arab garden to make a stew. That night, January 8, they slept in a hut and it was the best night they had known since December 30. Next morning they met an Arab policeman who led them towards the barracks and here they met three other members of their patrol. At 0130 hours. Major Steele arrived to take them in a truck back to Jalo, and the adventure was over.

In January Rommel's counter-offensive was making such progress that Jalo became rather uncomfortable and isolated. To their disgust the LRDG squadron was ordered to head back for Siwa, between the northeast shoulder of the Great Sand Sea and the Qattara Depression. And Stirling took his unit back to Kabrit.

Buerat and Benghazi

On arriving in Cairo Stirling put in a request to see Auchinleck. Though his unit had some proud achievements to its credit, the strength was down – Fraser and his party were still on their march across the desert – and more officers and men were needed if operations were to continue. Not having shaved since he reached civilisation, Stirling still wore a luxuriant beard which horrified some members of GHQ staff but impressed Auchinleck. At this precise moment the 8th Army was advancing yet again and any moment Benghazi was expected to fall. When this happened Rommel would have to utilise Buerat for his convoys, a small port lying beyond Tamet, some 350 miles to the west. So, asked by Auchinleck what he proposed to do next, Stirling suggested that he should attack the harbour at Buerat, sink any ships he found there, and destroy the dock installations. The raid could not take place before the middle of the month, when the moon had waned.

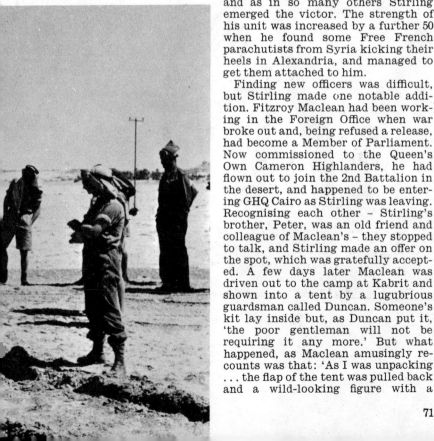

Recognising the extreme daring of the plan, Auchinleck gave his permission; he also authorised the recruitment of six officers and 30 men, and promoted Stirling to the rank of major.

So SAS were in business again; and eagerly Stirling set up a planning headquarters in his brother's flat in Cairo. Despite the fame of his unit throughout the Middle East theatre, (or perhaps because of it), there were still problems with the A and Q Staff, who produced a dozen reasons why this officer or that man should not be transferred, or why bombs or fuses or some other pieces of equipment had been allocated elsewhere. The Adjutant-General's branch were naturally enraged when Stirling invented a new cap badge for his unit, and pointed out – quite correctly, according to King's Regulations – that as the SAS was a mere detachment, his men should wear the badges and insignia of their own regiments. But in this scrap and as in so many others Stirling emerged the victor. The strength of his unit was increased by a further 50 when he found some Free French parachutists from Syria kicking their heels in Alexandria, and managed to get them attached to him.

Finding new officers was difficult, but Stirling made one notable addition. Fitzroy Maclean had been working in the Foreign Office when war broke out and, being refused a release, had become a Member of Parliament. Now commissioned to the Queen's Own Cameron Highlanders, he had flown out to join the 2nd Battalion in the desert, and happened to be entering GHQ Cairo as Stirling was leaving. Recognising each other – Stirling's brother, Peter, was an old friend and colleague of Maclean's – they stopped to talk, and Stirling made an offer on the spot, which was gratefully accepted. A few days later Maclean was driven out to the camp at Kabrit and shown into a tent by a lugubrious guardsman called Duncan. Someone's kit lay inside but, as Duncan put it, 'the poor gentleman will not be requiring it any more.' But what happened, as Maclean amusingly recounts was that: 'As I was unpacking ... the flap of the tent was pulled back and a wild-looking figure with a

beard looked in. "My tent" he said.' The figure was Bill Fraser, just arrived after his long march.

By January 10, Stirling's plans were made and the following morning he flew with his party to Jalo where they were joined by Captain Duncan and some men of the Special Boat Section, equipped with limpet mines and explosives. The raiding party was to be carried by a patrol of the LRDG under Captain A D N Hunter, with Michael Sadler as navigator, and was to leave on the 17th. The country towards Buerat was familiar to them by now, and no problems concerning the route were expected. It was necessary, however, to keep well to the south to avoid enemy reconnaissance planes, and several tyres were punctured on the rough ground. However, before dark on the 22nd the column reached the Wadi Tamet, some 50 miles from the objective, and Hunter decided that this obstacle must be crossed next morning. Camp was made on the edge of the Wadi and after dinner the signallers got through to Siwa at Stirling's request – he had hoped that information would be available from recent air reconnaissance photographs. In fact, the reply came that it would be available the following morning, which was a disappointment. Also there was the chance that in trying to obtain this data – which should have come days earlier while the column was in the desert – its presence would be disclosed.

Next morning Hunter decided that they must get down into the Wadi fast and take cover. As there was no time for a reconnaissance, the trucks went down at a precarious angle and it was fortunate that at least one of them did not overturn. No sooner were the trucks at the bottom and under their scrim nets than a plane came over and circled them before flying off north back to Tamet. They had been spotted. Immediately Hunter gave orders to disperse, and the trucks raced down the Wadi, looking for rocky overhangs or coves, the furthest penetrating five miles or more.

Half an hour later the bombers

Letter from home

arrived, six of them, and for an hour they flew up and down the Wadi bombing and machine-gunning. After this there was a respite until more aircraft arrived and the strafing began all over again. It was 1800 hours before Hunter could give orders for the column to concentrate again; and then it was found that although no one had been hit, the wireless truck and its operators had disappeared. What had happened? – whether it had gone too far south and been captured or blown up – it was impossible to say. But it was never seen again.

For Stirling especially, this was a great blow, for from now on he would be denied radio facilities and could receive no up-to-date information from base.

However, there was no turning back, and laboriously the trucks climbed of the Wadi and headed west to a point 65 miles from Buerat. Here the column stopped; the raiders hurriedly prepared their equipment, and Captain Duncan of the Special Boat Section began erecting his canoe.

Only one truck was to make the final journey to Buerat and on this had to be squeezed not only the canoe, but Hunter, Sadler, Duncan, Stirling and his 16 men. At 2045 hours they set off across the rough desert towards the tarmac road, knowing that once they had reached this there would be a 50 mile journey to their objective. But before they could even reach the road, there was trouble. Suddenly the front wheels of the truck went into a hole and the boat crashed against the side with a sickening sound of wood splintering. When they had stopped to examine the damage, it was found that the craft was split down the middle.

First the loss of surprise ... then the loss of the wireless truck ... and now this. The odds against success were stacking up rapidly and Stirling could have been excused for giving way to despair. In fact, he did no such thing; merely remarked that plans would be modified, and if the party could not get the ships out in the harbour, they'd concentrate on dock installations. One target was as good as another. The men accepted the decision cheerfully, remarking that there was more room on the truck without the canoe, and in a surprisingly cheerful atmosphere the party reached the tarmac road.

They could move faster now. In fact the remaining miles were covered in under the hour and then the truck drew up a few yards off the road. The time was just after midnight. Though nothing could be seen in the darkness except the bare earth stretching away, Michael Sadler was confident that Buerat was only a mile away. So they had two hours to get there, do their job and get back again for Hunter insisted that the truck must leave for the desert rendezvous by 0200 hours. Captain Duncan and his Corporal left first while Stirling split his men into two parties. One would go with him and the other with Sergeant-Major Riley, the plan being to approach the harbour from opposite directions. No one would use a gun unless they had to, and in fact, Stirling was insistent that their best weapon was stealth.

So they moved off and soon the desert gave way to a cultivated area. Though it was very dark they could make out the shapes of houses in the distance, and made a wide detour to avoid them, hoping to reach the harbour from the direction of the beach. The atmosphere was tense, for any moment they expected to bump a sentry or meet barbed wire or some other obstacle. But the place seemed empty. Also, no ships were riding at anchor and the only vessels of any kind that Stirling could find in a swift reconnaissance were a few fishing boats. Detailing a few men to stay on guard outside a large dockside building, he led the rest inside. Here they found some elaborate pumping equipment and placed their bombs on it. Further along they forced entry into a second building, which proved to be stacked high with crates of rations and supplies. Having dealt with these, Stirling led his party further round the harbour, only to bump into Sergeant-Major Riley and his men. Cursed for being in the wrong place, Riley said he had dealt with his targets – a food dump, machinery and a workshop but had then come up against a sentry post. He was now trying to get out of the harbour.

Both parties began to move away now, keeping closer to the road.

Spotting some large shapes in the darkness Stirling went forward to investigate, and found himself in the middle of a large transport park. Amongst the vehicles were several rows of petrol carriers, each with a capacity of 20 tons, and from the smell they appeared to have recently filled up. Calling up his men, Stirling dealt methodically with the carriers, and was just about to leave when he heard voices. But again it was Riley and his party who had also spotted the transport park and were working their way through it from the far end. To stop any further comic incidents of this nature, Stirling decided that the combined party should move back to the rendezvous together.

Hunter and the LRDG men were waiting as planned, and the only worry was concerning Captain Duncan and his corporal who had not yet returned from their job at the wireless station. Hunter decided he must leave now and come back for them the following night, so Stirling and his men clambered into the trucks and away they went. At 0240 hours the explosions started going off and the party gave a great cheer as they headed east. The enemy were short of petrol carriers and the night's work would make them shorter than ever. More shipping space would be required to bring over replacements – if indeed the vehicles could be replaced at all. Despite all hazards the raid had not proved abortive after all.

Next morning the planes were out after the raiders, but they remained parked in scrub with the scrim nets out. Then in the afternoon the sky clouded over, the wind rose and the sand began flying. Despite the discomfort, the party were almost glad – for aircraft could not possibly fly in this weather. At 2100 hours when the wind had dropped a good deal, Stirling went with Captain Hunter and a few men to try and pick up Duncan and his corporal. Again expecting trouble, they were relieved to spot a pile of sticks in the road – the agreed signal. Once the truck had stopped, Stirling leaped off and called out, to be answered by Duncan. He had dealt with the wireless station he said, placing a charge of 30-lbs of TNT in position. While getting away they had seen the

**Smoke in the desert: SAS patrol
watch enemy vehicle burning**

explosions and fires started by Stirling and his men around the harbor; 'It looked', Duncan said, 'as if a whole fleet of tankers had gone up.'

Feeling on the crest of a wave, Stirling decided to look for more targets before heading back for the desert, and found two more petrol tankers. Getting away after the explosions, however, the truck ran straight into an ambush and only escaped by the coolness of the driver who accelerated and drove straight on. Somehow the truck and its occupants managed to go straight through a curtain of machine-gun fire unscathed.

The following day the party remained hidden in the scrub and that night started back for Jalo.

One thing still puzzled Stirling. Why should the harbor have been empty?

What he did not know, through lack of radio communication, was that on January 21 Rommel had suddenly launched an attack which took the 8th Army completely by surprise. Within a week he was in Benghazi and in fact had re-taken the greater part of Cyrenaica. The 8th Army was back at its old position at Gazala.

Learning this news on the BBC Stirling decided that Jalo must be approached cautiously, as the Germans may have already sent a column to the place. In fact Captain Timson and G2 Patrol of the LRDG were still there, destroying dumps and laying booby traps. It was by a happy chance that the two parties did not start firing at each other. Having spent the night at Jalo the joint party left next morning for Siwa, and from there Stirling took his men back to Kabrit. Already new plans were forming in his head.

The most important of these was a

Road to Benghazi: there were also minor hazards

raid against Benghazi, again in full operation as Rommel's base and supply port. Indications at GHQ Cairo, were that Auchinleck could not mount an offensive for some months because of the slow build up of reserves and so would remain static at Gazala.

In this situation Stirling reasoned that, even though it took some weeks to plan, an operation between March 8 and 13 would be worthwhile. So details were worked out and raiding parties allocated to a number of targets in the Benghazi area. Stirling himself with Paddy Mayne and a party would tackle the airfields at Berka and Benina; a recently joined subaltern called Dodds would take on Slonta; and Bill Fraser, Barce. Stirling also had a wild idea of taking

some men from the Special Boat Section and driving into Benghazi harbor. Brigadier Marriott, with whom he discussed this idea, thought the whole thing wildly improbable. Benghazi would not be anything like Buerat, he said; there would be wire, roadblocks, and substantial defences in depth. However, after some persuasion, he agreed to put Stirling in touch with an Intelligence Officer called Gordon Alston who had a detailed knowledge of Benghazi. Alston agreed to go on the operation, as did two officers of the Special Boat Section, David Sutherland and Ken Allot. Finally Stirling recruited the services of a Belgian businessman, Captain Bob Melot, now working for the British Intelligence Service – he spoke fluent Arabic – and two Senussi soldiers.

Naturally there had to be close co-

blindfold: out of the Siwa depression, through the minefield at the base of the scarp, past a notice reading 'You are now entering a malarial area', across an old Royal Flying Corps landing ground of World War I, along the Sollum track for 80 miles, then the desert run to the southern flank of the Jebel mountains before continuing across the Tariq el Abd, then towards the Wadi Qattara and the escarpment dominating the Benghazi plain. Establishing a forward base in the foothills some 16 miles from the coast Stirling got Melot to brief two Senussis and send them out on reconnaissance. Meanwhile Paddy Mayne and a party set out for Berka airfield which lay a few miles to the south of Benghazi. The remainder of the party rested under the trees and enjoyed the cool water from the wells nearby. The scene was completely peaceful.

Next afternoon it was stirred into life, for the Senussis had come back reporting that there were no road-blocks along the main road to Benghazi. Taking Alston, Allot, together with two of his own men and two from the Special Boat Section, Stirling drove off in his staff car, escorted as far as the road by Olivey and the LRDG. Speeding along on the hard surface, Stirling could see groups of Arabs moving homeward after their day's work, but otherwise the road was clear. There was no sign of troops and the Senussi's report proved quite reliable. Soon the car reached the Arab quarters on the outskirts of the city and slowed down; then going on still unchallenged reached the European streets and the approaches to the harbor. Choosing a point about half a mile from the sea and outside the protective wire fence, Stirling stopped the truck among some bombed-out buildings. Then with Alston, Allot and two men he made his way along the back streets towards the sea. A strong wind was blowing and the air was cold; a complete blackout was in force throughout the area; and there was no sign of movement. They reached the water without incident.

But then came a snag. When Allot saw how choppy the sea had become, he expressed doubts as to whether the canoe could keep afloat. It certainly couldn't reach the ships which could

operation with the LRDG, and so Prendergast agreed that John Olivey and the Rhodesian patrol should carry the raiding party. At this time the patrol was based at Siwa which had become a great hive of activity. Constantly the LRDG were sending out patrols on 'road watch', dropping off spies towards the coastal road, reconnoitring Soluch and Sceleidima, or surveying the desert south of Jalo. On the airstrip Bombays and Lysanders, Wellingtons and Hudsons flew in and out in a steady stream. Never had this old and famous oasis known such noise and bustle.

The column left at daybreak on March 15, Stirling and his party travelling in a Ford Utility modified to resemble a German staff car, and Alston and Sutherland in a real one, captured a few months previously. The LRDG almost knew the route

be seen moored a hundred yards away. Suggesting that the canoe should be assembled in case the wind dropped, Stirling left for a quick look round the harbor. Except for a drunk he met no one at all, and was able to find a side entrance to the harbor which was not closely guarded.

Back at the water's edge, he found that Allot was having trouble with the canoe – some parts did not fit and so assembly could not be completed. Worse still, the wind had risen further and the waves were crashing against the pier then rising up a fury of white spume. There was no alternative but to give up, and so disgruntled and depressed the party went back to the car.

So the first Benghazi raid had failed. Back at the base among the foothills the news was equally depressing. Dodds had found the defences around Slonta airfield so heavy that it was impossible to get through. Alston lost his way to Berka and never got near the place. Bill Fraser got through to Barce but found only a single aircraft and some repair wagons which he blew up. The only cheerful news came from Paddy Mayne who came in with his two corporals reporting that he had blown up 15 aircraft near Berka. But he had troubles in getting back, having lost the way because of an inaccurate map. Later he wrote:

'The day and night after the raid we couldn't find our rendezvous . . . We had been walking from 0130 hours to 1900 hours the next night and couldn't find the damned place anywhere. We must have covered about 50 miles, first of all getting to the damned aerodrome and then coming away.

It was no good walking round in circles in the dark. I more or less reconciled myself to a 250 mile walk to Tobruk, and so we went to the nearest Senussi camp for some water and, if possible, a blanket.

The Senussi were very suspicious at first but once they were sure we were 'Englesi' everything changed and we were ushered into one of the tents, our equipment brought in, blankets put down for a bed.'

Lying awake in the darkness, Paddy pondered as to how he could ever find his way back to the rendezvous with the LRDG and Stirling. But then an extraordinary thing happened:

'And now listen to this, and never disbelieve in 'luck' again or coincidence, or whatever you like to call it. The men who were waiting for us at the rendezvous – and they would have left next morning – had got a chicken which they had bartered for some sugar. They wanted it cooked and they had an English-speaking Arab with them, so they sent him to get it cooked. In that area there must have been thirty or forty different encampments spread over the three odd miles we were from each other and he picked the one that we were lying in to come to – and so we won't have to footslog across the desert.'

Next day the column left for Siwa which was reached without incident. Though the destruction of aircraft was a notable achievement in itself, the operation had proved far, far less successful than Stirling had hoped. The memory of the boats riding at anchor only a hundred yards away remained to taunt him. If only the weather hadn't turned against him once more . . . if only the canoe hadn't proved a flop. The extraordinary thing was that the raid itself, the business of reaching Benghazi and getting away again, thought wild to the borders of insanity in Cairo, had proved so tame. He would definitely have another go.

Though the LRDG were now well established in their role as carriers for the SAS, it would be quite inaccurate to imply that this was their only or principal role. For every patrol co-operating with Stirling a dozen more were out on a variety of tasks, many routine but others of major importance and involving long journeys. On March 30, for example, one of the Guards patrols, under Captain the Honourable Robin Gurdon, left Siwa and, passing to the south of Jalo, which was now occupied by the Germans, covered 221 miles across the desert between sunrise and sunset, a remarkable feat by any standards. The following day they reached the New Zealand patrol, from which they took over road watch duties. The object was to note details of every type of vehicle moving along the road and signal it back to headquarters. From this data, Intelligence staff at 8th Army headquarters could work out the details of nemy intentions. Montgomery's Chief-of-Staff, General De Guingand wrote later that the LRDG road-watch reports 'proved most accurate and provided a first-class check on all other information concerning movement of troops and material.'

Despite their usefulness to the Army Staff, road-watch duties were hard and uncomfortable for the troops. Squatting in their holes under camouflage nets, they could only be relieved in the hours of darkness. There was danger, too, either of being spotted by enemy patrols of parties camping off the road, or being betrayed by the Bedouins. Sometimes the latter would resort to blackmail, demanding food

The pause before action: LRDG sergeant and driver

and money for keeping silent. On one occasion, when Gurdon's men had refused to be intimidated, a Bedouin walked across to a German officer and pointed to where the patrol was in hiding. But either failing to understand, or perhaps suspecting a trap, the officer did nothing.

After being relieved from the road-watch, Gurdon and his men left Siwa with Captain Melot, the Intelligence officer, and two Arabs who were to spy out the land south of Benghazi. He covered the journey of 430 miles in two days, another remarkable feat, and got back to base even faster. A few days later he was given his next job: to take a party of SAS back to Benghazi. This included Stirling, Fitzroy Maclean, and the Prime Minister's son, Randolph Churchill.

Benghazi again

Fitzroy Maclean was going on the raiding party because he had just completed his training and was a good linguist whose talents might come in handy. Randolph Churchill, a new recruit from GHQ Cairo, had not completed his training or even started it, but with his well-known powers of persuasion, had talked himself into a seat in the car. Apart from Stirling, the other members of the party were Gordon Alston, and three corporals who had been with SAS since its formation, Rose, Cooper and Seekings. Determined that there would be no failure this time because of the boat, Stirling had given the job of finding and testing the right article to Maclean; and Maclean managed to get hold of some reconnaissance boats from the Royal Engineers which were inflated with a pair of bellows. Stirling accepted these but insisted that some training must be carried out, so for several nights running the boats were taken down to the Great Bitter Lake

and put through their paces. As a final test Stirling suggested that Maclean take the boats to Suez and see if he could stick dummy limpet mines on British ships there, without being detected. The 'raid' went off just as successfully as the earlier affair at Heliopolis; and next day Stirling rang up the Port authorities to ask them for the return of his mines. The Royal Navy was not very amused.

One morning in mid-May the party left Kabrit in Stirling's staff car, with four machine-guns fitted on special mountings, two in front and two at the back. Their first call was at the Naval Intelligence Office in Alexandria where maps, air photographs, and the latest intelligence were made available, together with a wooden model of Benghazi. Seated silently before the latter, the raiders tried to memorise the necessary geographical details, noting a narrow stretch of shingle below the harbor jetties. Once past the sentries, this looked an ideal spot

Italian inf_____ the_____

from which to launch the boats. But what about entry into the town? Would this be as easy as last time? Opinion in Intelligence was that if an approach was made along the Benina road – that is from the east – there should be no problem. The check post sited on this route had recently been withdrawn.

After lunch the party piled back into the car and drove to Mersa Matruh, passing a sign post put up some years previously by the Royal Egyptian Automobile Club which read: 'BENGHAZI – 1000 km'. Next day they left Mersa Matruh on the two-day journey to Siwa, which Maclean was delighted to see, having heard stories about it since childhood. The place did not disappoint him and later he recorded his pleasure at the sight of the pools of fresh water bubbling up from a great depth under the palm trees. Following the example of his father a quarter of a century earlier, he plunged into one of the pools, and the experience he says 'was like bathing in soda water.'

Waiting for the party in LRDG headquarters, situated in some buildings, was Robin Gurdon, and conferences regarding the operation ahead began at once.

On the afternoon of the 18th the party left Siwa for Benghazi, and in the following days went on from dawn to dusk. Now the weather was hot and they stripped down to their shorts, glad of the breeze created by the movement of the trucks. Once the sun went down, of course, the temperature dropped rapidly and clothing would be piled on again. Regrettably, most men of action are not superb writers and the 'feel' of the vast majority of desert journeys has been lost or recorded fragmentarily. Fortunately Maclean is both man of action and writer and his famous work, *EASTERN APPROACHES*, has left a vivid account of these nights in the desert:

'Supper did not take long to prepare: hot bully stew, tea, and sometimes a tot of rum. It was cooked over a desert fire, made by pouring some petrol into a tin filled with sand, which then burned with a steady flame for a surprisingly long time. After we had eaten, and filled our water-bottles from the water-tank in preparation for the following day, we would sit round the fire muffled in our greatcoats. Sometimes when the day's signals had been sent and received, the wireless would be turned to more frivolous uses and we would listen to jazz music, or to Tommy Handley, or to the eight o'clock news from London . . . The continent of Europe seemed a long way away. I wondered when I would see it again and what it would be like by the time we got there.

Soon the fire would die down and we would seek out a soft patch of sand on which to spread out sleeping-bags. We slept soundly under the stars with a cool breeze playing on our faces.'

Before dawn the cook would be rattling his cans and shouting 'Come and get it!' and there would be the pulling on of boots and the day would begin. After a breakfast of porridge, sausage, and sometimes the delicious sliced bacon the army issued in tins, the journey would continue, first in cold air, but as the sun rose towards its zenith, the shedding of clothes would be repeated.

The desert was sometimes soft and sometimes stony, sometimes flat and at others undulating, but except for an occasional patch of coarse grass uniformally bare. The only sign of life was the tiny gazelles that went scampering into the distance, and a Beaufighter which flew overhead, ignoring the enemy recognition sign which Stirling's car carried. To the west of Gazala – where the German and British armies were now facing each other in the coastal strip – the routine was reversed, and the column travelled by night and lay up during the day. Usually it was possible to find some rocks or scrub to help the camouflage; but it was never possible to avoid the flies, which came to torment the men as they tried to get some sleep in whatever cover was available. The heat was almost unendurable.

Some 80 miles from Benghazi and running slap across the route, lay a caravan route called the Trigh-el-Abd. This was little more than a tangled skein of tracks strewn with the bones

Above: Tyre blow-out: the crew takes the chance to cook a meal. *Below:* Petrol and sand make an excellent stove

The Western Desert of Libya and Egypt – the playground of the Desert Raiders

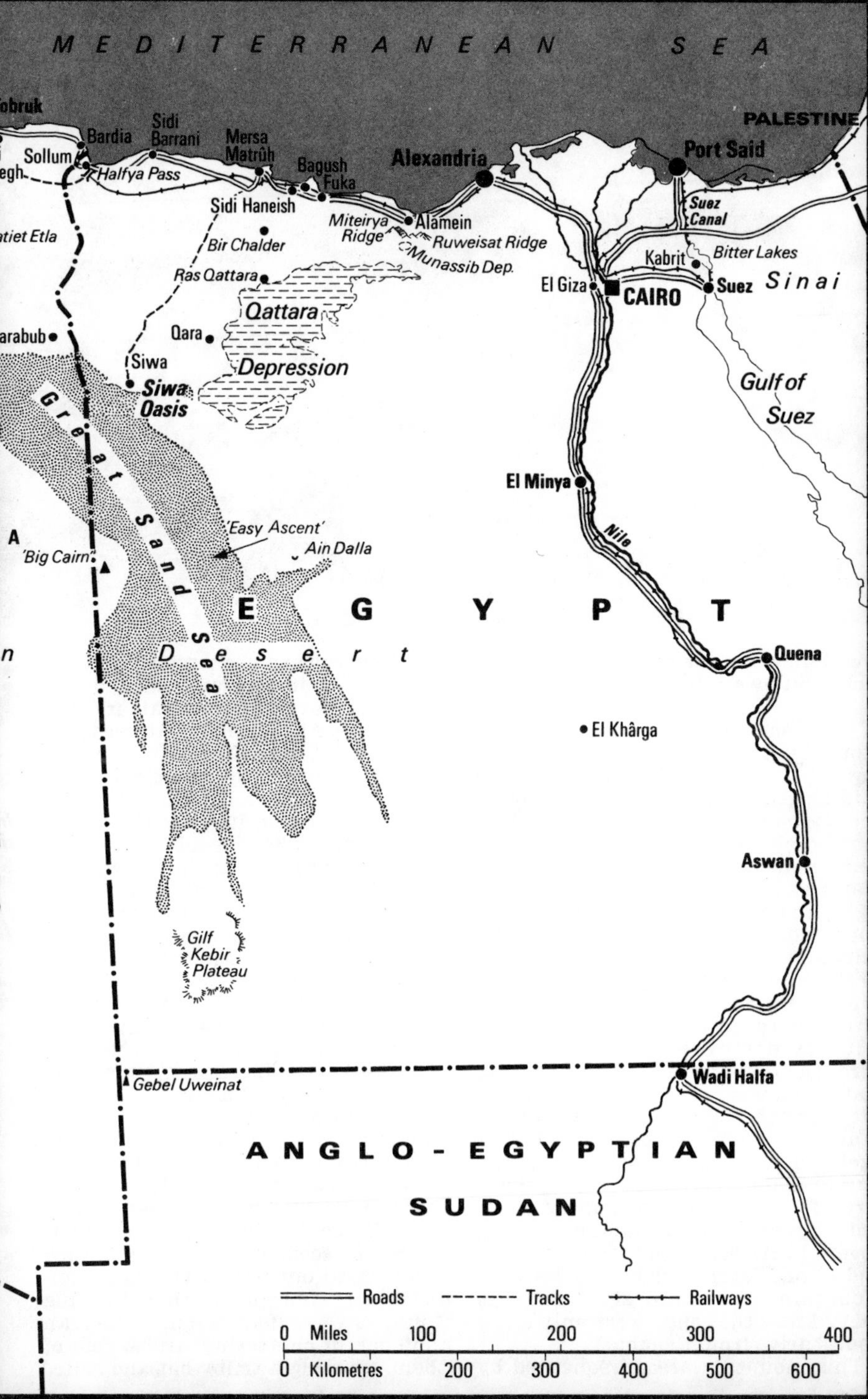

MEDITERRANEAN SEA

PALESTINE

Tobruk

Bardia
Sidi Barrani
Sollum
Halfya Pass

Port Said

Sidi Barrani
Mersa Matrûh
Bagush
Fuka
Alexandria

Suez Canal

ntiet Etla

Sidi Haneish
Bir Chalder

Miteirya Ridge
Alamein
Ruweisat Ridge
Munassib Dep.

Kabrit
Bitter Lakes

Ras Qattara

El Giza
CAIRO
Suez
Sinai

arabub

Qattara
Depression

Qara

Siwa
Siwa Oasis

Gulf of Suez

A
'Big Cairn'

'Easy Ascent'
Ain Dalla

El Minya

E G Y P T

n

Desert

Quena

El Khârga

Aswan

Gilf Kebir Plateau

Gebel Uweinat

Wadi Halfa

ANGLO - EGYPTIAN

SUDAN

| Roads | Tracks | Railways |

0   Miles   100   200   300   400

0 Kilometres   200   300   400   500   600

89

The Germans strike back: British trucks hit by artillery fire

of humans and camels which had died along it during many centuries. Knowing that it must be crossed by any raiding party approaching the coast, the Germans had strewn it with thermos bombs, which lay in great numbers, half-hidden by sand. Gurdon's plan was to approach the area at first light, and deal with the bombs as they appeared. This worked quite successfully and after an anxious half hour or so the column was through the danger zone and heading in a north-westerly direction towards the coast.

It was now that the raiders came across a startling reminder of the war and the dangers of their own escapade. Littering the sand were the wrecks of tanks and trucks, some with the skeletenous remains of their crews still in them. There were the wrecks of aircraft, too. Then the country changed from desert to hill and moorland, covered with scrub and stunted trees; and soon Jebel Akhdar, the Green Mountain, came into sight and the party knew that they were only a few hours' drive from Benghazi.

This mountain area, frequented by the Senussis and their roaming cattle and sheep, was well-watered, and gave excellent cover for the raiders' forward base. As mentioned already, the Senussis detested the Italians, and so the latter tended to keep clear of the area, as did their allies, the Germans. Carefully picking its way along goat tracks and *wadis*, the column reached a convenient point on the escarpment which it will be remembered, lies some 20 miles away from Benghazi across the plain. The date was now May 20 and the raid was timed for the following night. Lying in his sleeping bag, Fitzroy Maclean has recorded, he could see the flashes as the RAF bombed Benghazi. This was to be their last visit until Stirling and his men had been in and got out again.

Next morning the routine preparations were made: stores and ammunition were checked, guns were cleaned, equipment was tested, and the rubber boats were blown up, deflated, and carefully packed ready for transporting to the scene of action. This work was carried out not in the calm, undisturbed atmosphere that Stirling would have preferred, but before an audience of chattering Arabs. One of them, sporting a trilby hat and rolled

umbrella, spoke excellent Italian, and suspicions soon grew that he could be an enemy agent. However, by the time action against him had been decided upon, he had mysteriously disappeared.

Another job going on at this moment was the unpacking of explosives, the bombs and limpet mines, and fitting the detonators and timing gadgets to them. Though routine and familiar enough to the SAS this job always had to be done carefully and meticulously, for explosives are no respecters of persons. On this occasion there was a sharp crack, rather like a pistol going off, and Corporal Seekings was observed to be clutching his hand. A detonator had proved faulty and blown up as he held it. Though not badly hurt, he obviously could not go with the raiding party, so a jubilant Randolph Churchill – who was to have been left behind with Gurdon and the LRDG escort – talked Stirling into taking him in his place. No one doubted that if occasion warranted it, the newcomer would act with great courage, but there was a hope too that the famous Churchill voice would not boom out at the wrong moment.

Soon after 1700 hours Stirling and his five men – Gordon Alston, Fitzroy Maclean, Randolph Churchill, Corporal Rose and Corporal Cooper – set out for Benghazi, escorted by Gurdon and two trucks of the LRDG. In the growing darkness the column wound its way gingerly down a *wadi*, bumping and lurching over the rough ground and swerving violently on occasion to avoid large boulders. The going was so slow that five hours had passed before the 14-mile journey to the road had been completed.

At the road, the LRDG trucks turned back and Stirling, after a brief good-bye, switched his headlights full on and headed towards Benghazi. But once the car picked up speed, it soon became apparent that the rough ride down the *wadi* had had its effect, and one of the wheels had been forced out of alignment.

So there was a high-pitched shriek, and cursing his luck Stirling brought the truck to a halt off the road. For a while the Corporals lay on their backs under the car and tinkered, but nothing could be done. Painfully aware that his operation must be accomplished within the six hours of darkness, Stirling ordered them back into the car and drove off again, the noise worse than ever. Fitzroy Maclean felt rather as if he were in a fire engine racing to put out a blaze, rather than a supposedly elusive and clandestine raiding party. However, no one seemed to take any notice, and the only sign of life was the Arab camp fires twinkling like stars in the darkness. No barricades appeared, nor check posts. Soon the wire fence around Regima airfield could be seen on the right, and the party knew that Benghazi could not be far off. This realisation brought some relief, for apart from being noisy, the journey was a cold one, the night air cutting keenly through greatcoats and pullovers.

Then it happened. Rounding a bend Stirling observed a red light in the middle of the road about a hundred yards away. Jamming his foot on the brakes, he brought the car to a halt just before a heavy wooden bar, then observed a sentry with a tommy-gun approaching Maclean, sitting at the other end of the front seat. In the distance, supporting the sentry, could be seen the muzzles of several other machine-guns, and it was obvious that only bluff could succeed in getting the

Swamps: another hazard of the desert

party through. A shooting match was out of the question. Now the sentry was asking Maclean who exactly they were. 'Staff Officers' was the reply in Italian, 'and we're in a hurry.' For a moment the sentry stared suspiciously and peered round the car. Surely, it seemed, he must notice that the uniforms were British instead of Italian. However, after a few moments of suspense, he gave a half-hearted salute, remarking, 'You ought to get those headlights dimmed ', and opened the bar. With a screech the car continued its journey into Benghazi.

The next episode might have come out of any routine thriller, or Hollywood 'B' picture. A car came the other way with its headlights on, then turned hurriedly and gave chase. Possibly, the raiders thought, it was the military police patrol, warned by the check post to shadow the strange vehicle arriving by night. Stirling's reaction was to slow down and let the vehicle pass, but this it refused to do, keeping its distance. So he accelerated, then stopped and the other car did likewise. The only thing to do was race into Benghazi at 80 miles an hour, then turn down a side street, switch off the lights, and wait. What happened, of course, was that the other car raced

past and the sound of its engine faded into the distance.

But things got worse rather than better, for soon the sirens began sounding and, as the RAF had agreed to keep clear that night, it was pretty obvious that a general alarm was being sounded. This impression was reinforced as rocket after rocket shot into the sky and exploded. The staff car was more hindrance than help now, so Stirling decided to abandon it, and having removed all the equipment, left a bomb in the back with a time-pencil set at half an hour, and led his party through the ruins of the Arabs' quarter. Though people could be heard running in the distance, no one barred their path and it seemed that they might reach the water's edge without trouble. Then filing through a broken wall into a narrow street, they ran slap into an Italian Carabiniere. Again Maclean was equal to the situation. 'What is all this noise about?' he asked, to be told, 'Oh, just another of those damned English air-raids.'

Not appearing too anxious to break away, Maclean asked if it were not possible that the British were sending some ground forces against the town, only to be told with a chuckle that this was hardly likely since their army had been pushed back almost to the Egyptian frontier. Bidding the Carabiniere good night, the party went on its way – at least until he was out of sight. Then Stirling indicated that he wished to stop and re-consider. If opinion among the Carabiniere was that the sirens and rockets were only giving warning of an air-raid, perhaps the party was being too pessimistic. Why not get back to the car, remove the bomb, and so save themselves a long walk back to the rendezvous with Gurdon and the LRDG? By the time they reasoned the car a good 25 minutes had gone by and so the bomb was seized hurriedly and thrown over a nearby wall. Soon afterwards it went up.

The harbor was a mile away, so Stirling's orders were that Randolph Churchill and Corporal Rose should take the car away and hide it, while he, together with Fitzroy Maclean, Corporal Cooper and Gordon Alston as a guide should carry the boats and explosives in a kitbag. So they started, and soon their footsteps were echoing along the pavements of the European quarter; they felt very conspicuous and not a little apprehensive. By the wire fence protecting the harbor. Maclean spotted a sentry, and going up to him, said that his party's car had broken down, and they were looking for somewhere to spend the night. Could the sentry recommend anywhere? The sentry was not particularly helpful, but luckily he was not very observant either, and so the party tramped off to find a spot to get through the wire. In due course they found one, dragged their equipment through, then picked a route between cranes and railway trucks towards the water. When they reached this, it was gratifying to observe that the spot on the shingle was exactly the one chosen from the model in Alexandria. Now Stirling decided to divide the party temporarily, taking Alston with him to reconnoitre the harbor, while Maclean and Corporal Cooper inflated the boat.

There was no moon, but the stars were bright and visibility was uncomfortably good. The surface of the water, so Maclean has recorded, 'was like a sheet of quicksilver' and what seemed a short distance across it

The Bedouin: sometimes friend, sometimes enemy

German Heavy Armoured Car Sd Kfz 234/3
Speed: 53 mph. *Range:* 372 miles. *Crew:* 4. *Armament:* One 7·5 cm L/24 Cannon,
one 7·92 mm machine gun.

German Light Armoured Car Sd Kfz -222
Speed: 50 mph. *Range:* 180 miles. *Crew:* three. *Armament:* One 20-mm cannon,
one 7.92-mm machine -gun

could be seen the hulks of the ships riding silently at anchor. The bellows made a squeak and, worse still, failed to inflate the boat. Maclean made a swift check of the connections and began pumping again, to be interrupted by a voice from one of the ships, wanting to know what was going on. 'Militari' he called back, but the owner of the voice was far from satisfied and wanted to know what was going on. In an assured voice Maclean shouted 'Nothing to do with you' and after this there was a merciful silence.

But the boat remained flat, and quite obviously must have been punctured, since the inspection that morning; the only course was to fetch the other boat from the car. Making their way back, Maclean and Cooper found Randolph Churchill trying to ease the vehicle into the cover of a bombed-out building, before a group of appreciative Arabs. Grabbing the boat, they got back through the wire and down to the water, but no sooner had begun pumping than to their horror they found that this craft also had been punctured. Soon Stirling and Alston returned, to be told the bad news. All the tooing-and-froing had eaten up the hours of darkness, and now there was only half an hour left. For a few moments the raiders debated whether to plant their bombs in the railway trucks, but decided that as targets were not sufficiently important to merit prejudicing a full-scale raid on the harbor. The operation must be written off as a failure.

It was a bitter moment. There was no time to sit and reflect, however, for if all traces of the visit were to be erased, the boats and equipment had to be collected and taken back to the car. At one point Maclean found himself face to face with an Ascari from Italian Somaliland, and again had to use his wits and linguistic expertise to get away without raising suspicions. But now the episode began to take on the aspect of a Hitchcock thriller, for trudging towards the wire with their kitbags the raiders suddenly discovered their numbers had grown from four to six. Two armed sentries had fallen in behind them. What was to be done? To shoot them would have meant rousing all the troops in the area; and yet it was impossible to try

and creep through the wire. The only course was to head straight for the main gate and trust that yet again some form of bluff could be worked.

At moments like these, as anyone knows who has been in a tight corner, the mind races ahead and operates with crystal clarity. Correspondingly, time appears to be stretched so that even a single pace can occupy an agonising aeon of time. By the time the party had reached the gate, Maclean was quite clear as to his course: in Italian he told the sentry to fetch the guard commander. Soon that individual, a sergeant, appeared, hurriedly buttoning up his trousers. Maclean informed him that he was an officer on the General Staff and asked if he was responsible for harbor security. When the sergeant sheepishly admitted that he was, Maclean berated him soundly. How was it he asked that he and his party could wander about the harbor unchallenged? It was outrageous. For all the sergeant knew, they might be enemy saboteurs. The Italian thought this a bit far fetched, but to his relief Maclean informed him that he would be let off this time – though he had better smarten up his sentry.

With this Maclean set off through the gate at a brisk walk, followed by the others. It had been a narrow shave.

It was daylight when the raiding party got back to the car and quite obviously all chances of an immediate return to the rendezvous were gone. Randolph Churchill and Corporal Rose had succeeded in getting the vehicle inside a half demolished house, and by using any materials that happened to be to hand, it proved possible to camouflage it fairly effectively. But where was the party to hide? Fortunately the rooms above the car were empty and with a bit of luck, it was thought, they could lie up in them throughout the day. There was food in the car and rum available, so things might have been far worse, though whether the Arabs would give them away it was impossible to guess.

With daylight the town began to wake up. German and Italian bombers roared back from the front. The local inhabitants, who had spent the night outside the city to avoid the bombing now flooded back to cook breakfast.

The Breda 8-mm machine gun: this weapon, the standard Italian medium machine gun, was so reliable that on the rare occasions that they could capture both gun and ammunition the Desert Raiders used it in preference to their own Lewis gun

Looking across the other side of the road Stirling even spotted the German sub-area headquarters, with officers bustling in and out, and signallers leaving with messages. The suspense could hardly have been greater.

But the day wore on and nothing happened. In turn the six men went on watch while the rest dozed. For Stirling it was a most unhappy day. Twice he had reached the harbor and twice the boats had let him down. Why should this be? What had happened? Was there a mystique about boats that he had failed to penetrate? The sun climbed to its zenith then slowly eased down towards the west. Not until Randolph Churchill went on watch near tea-time did anything happen – and then footsteps were heard on the stairs and an Italian sailor appeared. Confronted with Churchill and a six-day beard he beat a hurried retreat, but whether his intention was to inform the authorities it was impossible to say. However, for two hours the raiders sat tense with guns at the ready and grenades in hand, determined to give any further intruders a hot reception.

No one came, and the conclusion was that the sailor must have been after loot. But it was a great relief when darkness came down.

With all quiet again, Stirling led the party from their hiding place to make a tour of the city. He was still loathe to leave without inflicting some damage, and on reaching the water's edge was delighted to find two motor-torpedo boats tied up alongside the quay. Without hesitation he decided that it was worth having a go at them and quickly led his men back to the car for some bombs. But it was no use. By the time they returned sentries were in position, and far more alert sentries than had been encountered before. Eventually Stirling had to give up, and drive out of the town the way he had come, along the Benina road. Again Maclean had to talk his way past the road block, and even after this, the car had to travel some distance sandwiched between the trucks of a convoy. It was 0600 hours when they reached the rendezvous with Gurdon a day late, and the LRDG were just having breakfast before moving off.

Within the hour the journey to Siwa was begun, and some days later was accomplished without incident. The same cannot be said for the journey from Siwa to Cairo, for going at speed, Stirling managed to overturn the car; Maclean fractured a collar bone and broke an arm, Churchill crushed a vertebra and had to be invalided home, and Corporal Rose had a compound fracture of his arm. Stirling himself cracked a bone in his wrist which prevented his driving, even if he kept out of hospital. Altogether it was a disastrous end to an abortive expedition. But Stirling was determined to return to Benghazi yet again. He detested failure.

Nothing ahead except the desert and the enemy: a patrol leaves base

Save Malta

The spring of 1942 was a most anxious time for the Allies, and especially for Winston Churchill. Since February he had been watching the worsening situation on Malta, the British bastion in the Mediterranean, and urging Auchinleck to launch an offensive in the desert. Auchinleck kept replying that he could not attack until his men and supplies were up to strength, causing Churchill to ask sarcastically what he was doing with the 650,000 men already on the ration strength. On April 20 General Dobbie signalled Churchill from Malta, 'The very worst may happen if we cannot replenish our vital needs, especially flour and ammunition, and that very soon . . . it is a question of survival.' Presented with this news Auchinleck still dug his toes in and refused to move, arguing that the risks were too great. Churchill came back yet again, pointing out that the loss of Malta would be 'a disaster of the first mag-

nitude for the British Empire and probably fatal in the long run to the defence of the Mediterranean.' To strengthen his hand, he also obtained the full backing of the Chief-of-Staffs committee and the cabinet and so was able to inform Auchinleck that unless he attacked by mid-June at the latest, when, in the moonless period, a convoy of 17 ships would be approaching Malta, he must quit his command. Auchinleck submitted but already had delayed too long: on May 26 Rommel loosed one of his lightning offensives and five days of heavy fighting, ensued, after which Auchinleck mistakenly imagined that Rommel had shot his bolt. It was at this juncture on June 2 that Churchill signalled Auchinleck: 'There is no need for me to stress the vital importance of the safe arrival of our convoys at Malta, and I am sure you will both take all steps to enable the air escorts and particularly the Beaufighters, to be operated from landing-grounds as far west as possible.

It was against this background that, on his return to Cairo, Stirling found himself summoned to GHQ where he was interviewed by the Director of Military Operations. A convoy of merchant ships, he was told, would attempt to get through to Malta with their precious cargoes, in the second week of June. Every method must be used to reduce and neutralise the enemy threat from the air, and the help of SAS was urgently needed. What could be done? It did not take Stirling very long to evolve his plan, and this was to raid eight enemy airfields on the night June 13/14. Of these airfields two would be in the Benghazi area, three round Derna and Martuba, which lay on the coast about 100 miles west of Tobruk, one at Barce, and the last at Heraklion on the island of Crete.

The operation, as will be evident, was a complicated one, and time was short. At the base in Kabrit the activity went on from morning to night with plans being re-drafted as new Intelligence reports came in, were scrapped and drafted again. The Derna raids, to be led by Lieutenant Jordan of the Free French, presented special problems, for, apart from the distance involved, it was known that this hilly area was packed with German reinforcements and line of communications units. Fortunately Stirling learned about a unit called the SIG – The Special Interrogation Unit as it was called for security purposes – which consisted of a small group of German Jews, from Palestine. These brave men, risking almost certain death, had volunteered to go behind the German lines wearing Afrika Korps uniforms. Their training was

Men of the LRDG and comrades from the Free French Forces: the French desert fashions were not from Paris

thorough in the extreme and, so they should even think in contemporary German slang, their commander, Captain Herbert Buck MC recruited two German NCOs who had served in the French Foreign Legion and proclaimed themselves to be passionately anti-Nazi. The names of these men were Brückner and Esser, and though they worked admirably, the other members of the SIG never trusted them and considered their recruitment a bad mistake. The extent to which they were justified will be seen in due course.

Stirling was the first to call on the services of SIG and Buck was delighted

to meet him. The idea put forward was that SIG should produce three Afrika Korps trucks and drive the French patrols on to airfields around Derna. This, so Buck thought, should be quite simple, and suggested that the two parties rendezvous at Siwa on June 8. However, Stirling, who knew too well how long preparations for a raid could take, suggested an earlier date, and so it was arranged.

On June 6 the raiders set out led for the first four days by an escort of the LRDG. Then the SIG men put on their German uniforms and prepared to head for Derna. Everything had gone smoothly except for one important

detail – Intelligence had supplied the password for May (which was *Fiume*) but failed completely to ascertain the new one for June. This might easily make things very difficult, but there was no drawing back, and so the column headed north towards the mountains. Buck was dressed as a private, and Brückner and Esser as NCOs; and the Free French crouched in the back of the trucks under a tarpaulin. Every man was heavily armed, not only with pistols and sub-machine-guns, but with sharpened bayonets and grenades.

All the morning the trucks rumbled forward, and then on into the afternoon. At about 1600 hours, when rounding a bend, Buck saw a check barrier ahead, with a guardroom by it and sentries on duty. Driving up to it, he demanded that the barrier should be lifted and for a moment it looked as if the Italian sentry would do as bid. Then he hesitated and demanded the password, to which Buck replied that he had left on a desert mission before the old password 'Fiume' had been changed. Playing his role superbly, Buck flourished his forged orders in the sentry's face, but failed to budge him, and then to make matters worse, a major arrived who asked the 'Germans' into the guardroom to discuss the position over a glass of wine. Accepting the invitation, Buck explained that his job was to deliver the trucks to the workshops at Derna as quickly as possible, but the major was obviously very worried, repeating that his orders were explicit: no one could come through who could not give the password. Finally Brückner pretended to lose his temper and threatened to make a report to his unit that Italian sentries were obstructing important business. So the major gave way.

Climbing back into his vehicle Buck was accosted by a German corporal and expected more trouble, but the latter was only trying to be helpful. It would be wiser, he said, to pull up at the staging post a mile down the road and stay the night there. The danger from enemy saboteurs who came in from the desert and shot up vehicles should not be ignored . . .

So it was that half an hour later, Buck and his men found themselves queueing up among Luftwaffe and

Afrika Korps men for a supper of lentils and dumplings while the French stayed silent in the trucks. But he did not wish to push his luck too far, and an hour later the column moved out of the staging camp and halted seven miles further along the road. Here it spent the night undisturbed.

The following day was June 13 and the raids were planned to take place that night. Obviously the next task was to get the password and so the two NCOs from the Foreign Legion were sent to a nearby German post to ask boldly for it.

To the relief of Buck and Jordan they succeeded without difficulty: the challenge was *Siesta* and the reply *Eldorado*. By noon Buck moved the column to a point within five miles of Derna airfield which was to serve as the rendezvous. The next task was to take Jordan and his party to have a look at the area, and the method selected was to keep them concealed in the truck while it moved around, their vision limited to what they could see through a small hole, in the fabric. Jordan naturally wanted to reconnoitre all four airfields (two at Derna and the others at Martuba) but Buck's judgment was that the risks were too great, and only the first two were skirted. Just before dark the party got back to the rendezvous without incident.

Now Jordan gave out his orders. Corporal Tourneret and four men would take on one of the Martuba airfields; Jordan and Corporal Bourmont would lead four men each and head for the Derna airfields. Both parties would go in the same lorry driven by Brückner who would drop off Jordan first and then the other party.

To Jordan the truck seemed to be moving too slowly and an hour had gone by before five miles were covered. Then Brückner stopped the truck near Derna cinema, remarking that the engine was overheating and he had lost the key to the tool chest. With this he walked over to the guardroom, presumably to get another, but then Jordan heard the sound of footsteps and in a flash the vehicle was surrounded by troops. 'All Frenchmen out' came the cry, and to his horror Jordan realised that his early suspicions had been justified, and the party was betrayed.

But the Frenchmen weren't taking things quietly. One of them flung a grenade and others began firing their sub-machine guns. The Germans scattered and Jordan, breaking free of the men who had hauled him from the truck, ran for his life. A few seconds later there was a great explosion and looking back he could see that the truck was enveloped in flames. One of the SIG finding himself trapped in the vehicle, had flung a grenade into the explosives. Two hours later Jordan got back to the rendezvous and told Buck the bad news.

What was to be done? Obviously any survivors would not come to this place, but to the LRDG rendezvous 25 miles back. So the two men got away at once and linked up with the LRDG before dawn. For the next seven days they waited for stragglers but none came. Later they learned that all had been killed or captured.

Brückner was flown to Berlin where Hitler awarded him the *Deutsche Kreuze* in gold.

While Jordan and his men were at Derna, Stirling, Paddy Mayne, and Lieutenant Zirnheld led their men against the three principal airfields at Benghazi, having made the desert journey once more with Robin Gurdon's patrol of the LRDG. With Stirling on this job were the faithful corporals, Cooper and Seekings, and the party moved on foot. Their target was Benina airfield which was being used by the Germans as a repair base, and, (as they had seen during the previous day), the place was crowded with workshops and hangars. There was no wire round the field, and walking in the darkness they were about to get on to it unchallenged. Then there came the sound of aircraft and to his horror Stirling realised that, despite a firm promise to stay away on this particular night, the RAF were here for an airstrike. Soon the sticks of bombs came hurtling down and there were explosions all over the field. Nothing much was hit, and indeed most of the bombing was very inaccurate, but apparently satisfied the planes went away again.

Getting to their feet unscathed, Stirling and his men approached the hangars where sentries could be seen

The Opera House, Valetta, Malta:
destroyed by German bombers, April
1942

patrolling. Choosing his moment, he motioned to the corporals and they crept into a darkened hangar which proved to be packed with machinery and repair equipment. Working swiftly each time the sentry outside went to the far end of his beat, the party stuck on their bombs, then moved to the next hangar – a lighted one. Here posting the corporals on watch by the door, Stirling moved round putting on more bombs, some of them only a few yards from a group of German technicians working on machinery. In a third hangar they found two JU 52 bombers and about 40 crated aero engines, and Stirling had almost finished sticking on his bombs when the Germans began changing the guard. For a while it looked as if the raiders would be blown up by their own bombs – Stirling was now using 30-minute fuses – but somehow they managed to slip away. Then, with great daring, Stirling pulled the pin from a grenade, opened the door of the guardroom, and called to the commander seated at the desk, 'Here catch this.' Petrified the German caught the bomb, crying 'Nein, nein!' and as Stirling closed the door and ran there was a big explosion. A few seconds later and from a safe distance on the perimeter, the three men turned back as great explosions rent the air. One by one the hangars went up with the aircraft inside them, and the flames could be seen for miles. The raid, carried out by only three men with 60 Lewes bombs, had been a triumphant success.

Meanwhile Paddy Mayne with Corporal Lilley and two men called Warburton and Storey were busy at Berka. Having got on to the airfield without trouble they found themselves being bombed by the RAF and the whole place came alive, with anti-aircraft fire going up and flares floating down. One of the RAF planes was hit and crashed not far from the raiders. After what seemed to be an age the RAF departed, and Paddy Mayne decided he had better get a move on. Corporal Lilley has recorded:

'Paddy sent me forward to put a bomb on the nearest plane. I was challenged by a sentry standing under the wing of the aircraft. I dropped to the ground as he fired and at the same time Paddy threw a grenade. There was a flash and the sentry seemed to part in mid-air. There were other sentries by the plane. They fired and for a few minutes there was a pitched battle . . . We decided to crawl away and leave them . . . Several times, as we made our way off the airfield, we were fired at but before we left we managed to put our bombs on a large petrol dump.'

While this was going on, Captain Zirnheld and his men were fighting a pitched battle at Berka main airfield, and before it was over had destroyed eleven bombers and killed the troops guarding them. Another French party under Jaquier dealt with petrol and supply dumps at Barce.

With the information gained from Brückner the Germans realised, of course, that all the incidents were part of a highly planned operation and soon had ordered out mobile columns to deal with the raiders. Paddy Mayne and his party, walking back to the escarpment, bumped into one of these columns and were forced to lie flat on their faces for over two hours. As daylight came Paddy decided that the party must split up and moved off with Storey, leaving Lilley and Warburton. The latter decided to run for it and was picked off by a machine-gun, and Lilley, having laid in hiding for some hours, decided the best course was to dump his kit and walk through the lines of the German camp in which he found himself, in his shirt and shorts. He records:

'I walked for a couple of miles beyond the encampment until I reached the railway line that crosses the Benghazi plain. It was a deserted spot and the only sign of life were Arabs in the far distance working in the fields. I was near the road which runs parallel with the railway and suddenly I saw an Italian soldier coming along on a pushbike. He slowed up when he saw me, staring at me very hard. Then he got off his bike and came over to me leaving his rifle on the crossbar. He indicated that I was his prisoner and that I had to go back with him to Benghazi.'

But Lilley had no intention of being taken captive and grappled with the Italian, eventually succeeding in strangling him. Walking on, he reached a Senussi camp, where two hours later he was told that two soldiers were approaching. Looking up he saw Paddy Mayne and Storey. That night the three men climbed the Benghazi escarpment and next morning rejoined Stirling and his party.

One might think that the hair-raising escapes and adventures of the last few days had slaked Stirling's and Mayne's thirst for danger, but not a bit of it. Borrowing an LRDG truck from Robin Gurdon the two officers took five men and headed for Benghazi. Their object was to see what damage they had caused the night before, and shoot up anything they fancied along the road. Before long they had bumped into a German check post with barbed wire and a barricade and were asked to give the password. Naturally they could only give the old one, but the sentry, hearing the safety catches go off on the sub-machine-guns, decided that discretion was the better part of valour and let them through. But as the party realised, he must have telephoned to his unit farther down the road, and it was pointless to try and enter Benghazi itself.

However, they were soon opposite a transport filling station with large tanks on which they planted bombs. From here they went to deal with heavy lorries and trailers and shot up a camp near the road. The route they chose for their return was across the Wadi Qattara which runs parallel with the road, but the trouble was that there was only one crossing point, some five miles away, and so they had to travel on a compass bearing. Before long another vehicle appeared with the obvious intention of heading them off, and the only course was to put the headlights on and drive the truck at full speed across the bumpy ground. It was a nightmare journey with the passengers hanging on for dear life, but soon it was plain that they had a slight lead on the enemy. But what worried them was whether they had hit the right spot on the Wadi, for a mistake would mean disaster. For a while it looked as if they had done, and Paddy Mayne veered right along the edge, with the German a few hundred yards behind him. Then Stirling spotted the place and gave a loud yell,

and swinging the wheel Mayne made for the crossing. They were just in time. Later Corporal Seekings wrote, 'Luckily the Jerries dropped the chase, they were no doubt windy of being ambushed if they ventured down the narrow defile. We finally reached the escarpment.'

But the night's adventures were not over yet. On the way back to the rendezvous there was the smell of smoke and Lilley realised that a fuse was burning. Hurriedly the party leapt from the truck – barely a second before they jumped there was a loud explosion and it was blown to pieces. According to Lilley 'What was left of it you could have put in a haversack.' That night the men stayed in a Senussi camp, and Stirling persuaded the headman to send a message to Robin Gurdon requesting transport to be sent. Next day they reached the relative safety of the rendezvous, then began the journey back to Siwa.

It was some weeks before Stirling learned the details of the Crete raid, which was led by the Frenchman Berge and the most recent recruit to SAS, Lord Jellicoe, son of the famous admiral. After some amazing adventures they had managed to destroy no less than 21 planes, apart from petrol dumps and various installations. So with the 11 destroyed by Zirnheld at Berka, and the five destroyed by Stirling himself – apart from 30 engines and workshop installations – the operation had been a considerable success.

Sad to relate, only two ships got through to Malta out of the entire convoy, but their cargoes managed to keep the island fighting for two months until five more ships got through.

Also sad to relate, by July Rommel had pushed back the 8th Army yet again to its last defence line at El Alamein. And Tobruk, the bastion which had held out so long, fell to the enemy, with vast quantities of stores. The Royal Navy – as a precaution – pulled out of Alexandria. The Royal Air Force pulled back its bomber bases to Palestine. And in Cairo the staff at GHQ burned thousands of documents. After two years of fighting, and the expenditure of many lives and great effort, the situation seemed as bad as it had ever been.

Verbal orders: Rommel with a group of his officers

The jeep raid

In Cairo and London and elsewhere there was great depression. But Stirling refused to be depressed and in fact infused his unit with greater enthusiasm than ever. Now was the time, he argued, to set up a semi-permanent base behind the enemy lines and make a series of raids on their airfields. So on July 2 the unit left Kabrit and wound its way west along the rim of the Qattara depression before heading north along the track from Qara to Mersa Matruh. Here at a spot among the hills some 70 miles from the coast, the SAS and two LRDG patrols under Gurdon and Timpson lived for the next few weeks. During this time they blew up pipelines west of Matruh and raided airfields around Fuka.

On July 8 Robin Gurdon was with Zirnheld on the coast road near Fuka, where they destroyed transport and fuel tankers. Three days later, trying to repeat the operation, the column was caught just before dark by three

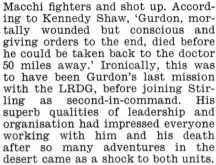

Macchi fighters and shot up. According to Kennedy Shaw, 'Gurdon, mortally wounded but conscious and giving orders to the end, died before he could be taken back to the doctor 50 miles away.' Ironically, this was to have been Gurdon's last mission with the LRDG, before joining Stirling as second-in-command. His superb qualities of leadership and organisation had impressed everyone working with him and his death after so many adventures in the desert came as a shock to both units.

Never content to sit back and rely on past techniques, Stirling was now experimenting with a new method of attacking airfields. His idea was to employ jeeps – each with a driver and two gunners to handle the four Vickers guns – and advance in formation. Led by Stirling, the jeeps would drive round the airfield pouring out a mixture of tracer and incendiary bullets which would destroy any aircraft in range. So, having left thirty men at the rendezvous near Qattara he went to Cairo, to get the necessary equipment, and eight days later was back with 20 jeeps, some 3-ton trucks and much needed supplies. He also had a plan – to try out his new theory with an 18-jeep raid against Sidi Haneish, the Germans' principal staging area near Fuka.

First there had to be rehearsals, so the jeeps drove out into the desert by night in two columns five yards apart. Stirling himself with his navigator, Michael Sadler, led the force, his jeep being midway between, and slightly in advance of, the column leaders. When he fired a Very light, the jeeps fanned out to take up a V formation then opened fire to a flank. With so many guns in vehicles as small as jeeps there was a danger of the drivers' being shot up and they had to keep very still, even when manoeuvring their vehicles over bumpy ground. To bend forward or lean back meant getting their head blown off. Fortunately though, the rehearsals went on until Stirling was satisfied, there were no accidents.

On July 26 all was ready, and just after sundown the jeep force left the desert base near Bir Chalder and headed towards Sidi Haneish, some 40 miles to the north-west. Steve

Jeep raiders line up for action

Digging out

Hastings who was on the raid recorded later:

'It was easy to see at first. We kept to no particular formation and the drivers just picked their own way a little to right or left of the man in front and followed his dust; occasionally a jeep would hit a rock or a bad bump and the gun mountings would rattle and the cans and ammo. boxes clash in the back. Mostly we rolled along at a good 20 mph over flat shingle or sand. Every now and again we would come to small escarpments and then bunch together until we found a way up or down. The dust rose thicker and engines revved as they changed gear. They would pull up one after the other and fan out again on the level.'

By the time they reached the Siwa track the moon was up, and Stirling called a halt while Sadler fixed his theodolite on its mounting and took a bearing. His was a great responsibility for it was necessary to hit the airfield plumb on. Any miscalculation and both time and surprise would be lost. But all seemed well, so the columns moved on again and the country became rougher. Jeep after jeep got a puncture and, as each of these took five minutes or more to fix, a good hour was lost. Then a cliff loomed up in the darkness, running slap across the line of advance. How was this to be negotiated? Sending off jeeps right and left to reconnoitre, Stirling was able to find a *wadi* and up this the jeeps slithered and lurched till they managed to reach the top. By now the journey had been going on for three hours and there was another halt to check weapons and make last minute preparations. By Sadler's calculations Sidi Haneish was just ten miles to the north.

They drove towards it over rolling country, and the moon began hiding behind the clouds so that unidentifiable shadows moved across the landscape. Soon there were the usual signs

touched down, was almost on it. Immediately he opened fire and the sixty-eight machine-guns in the jeeps behind him followed suit. There was a great roar and the tracer bullets raced across the ground in a sort of crazy firework display. A Very light – and the jeeps fanned out into their V formation, still going fast across the tarmac. Ahead Stirling could see rows and rows of planes – Stukas, Heinkels, and Junkers 52.

Half Rommel's airforce seemed to be on parade, a magnificent target. At close range the tracer poured in and one by one the aircraft began to blaze. Soon it seemed as if the whole airfield was alight and in the distance enemy soldiers could be seen running towards their defence posts. A mortar shell came down behind Stirling's jeep and then a Breda cannon opened up. To quote Hastings again:

'I felt something hot pass beneath my seat. There was a clang, and my face and that of my front gunner were covered in oil. There was a moment of blindness and incomprehension; we wiped the oil out of our eyes and the jeep swerved violently, hit a bump, recovered itself and continued miraculously!'

At the same time Stirling's jeep was put out of action and the force came to a standstill. While another jeep came to pick him up, he told the gunners to concentrate on the Breda, which was soon silenced. When all the engines were switched off Stirling gave new orders. They would complete the circle of the airfield dealing with any planes they came across, then get away. So the engines revved up again and the formation moved forward, only firing now as each target presented itself. Most of the remaining planes proved to be JU 52s and these were all dealt with, Paddy Mayne running over to the last one and placing a bomb in it to make sure.

The first jeep raid was over. The problem now was to get back over the desert, avoiding the vengeance of the Luftwaffe which would surely arrive with the dawn. Three jeeps had been knocked out and six hit, but fortunately the latter were still running.

Stirling's orders now were that the force would break up, each party getting as far as it could before day-

that the column had reached the coastal strip – burnt-out trucks and the debris of battle. Then there came the signs of habitation.

Here Stirling stopped his force, reckoning that the objective was about a mile off and straight ahead. Nothing could be seen and the whole area was silent. Either the airfield had gone dark or it was remarkably well concealed. However, Stirling gave a curt order and the jeeps formed into their double column and slowly moved over the broken ground. Then suddenly the men had a shock, for there in front of them a bare half a mile away was the airfield – flood-lit from end to end. What had happened? Had the Germans somehow got wind of their arrival? Was the game up? In a few seconds they had their answer, for a bomber came in to land.

At this moment Stirling showed his superb qualities of leadership, for without showing a flicker of hesitation he headed straight for the flare-path and by the time the bomber

light, then camouflaging its jeeps and hiding up. The following night the parties would head for the rendezvous by any route they chose. Checking up, it was found that there was only one casualty – a front gunner, hit by the mortar bomb. Stirling decided to take his body in his own party, which comprised four jeeps and 14 men.

He drove as fast as he dared, knowing that whatever happened they must reach cover. One of the jeeps gave out, so the spare wheel and the petrol were removed and it was blown up. Crowded on to the three remaining jeeps the party drove on again, covering about 30 miles by the time the sky grew light to the east. The desert continued bare, with no sign of cover whatever, but mercifully for half an hour or so there was a ground mist which hid the trucks from the air. Then, when it was almost too late the party found themselves on the edge of a small escarpment, dropping some fifteen feet to a large depression. And in the depression were patches of scrub.

Quickly the jeeps were manoeuvred into the scrub, the scrim nets were put over them, then clumps of scrub were uprooted and thrown on to the nets, until the vehicles were invisible even from a few yards. The strain was

Right: A scorpion on his beret; soldier of the LRDG *Below:* German desert patrol

relaxed. And after a mug of tea had been drunk, the dead gunner was buried in the sand. Then there was time to sleep. No aircraft bothered the party though Stukas flew overhead, and firing could be heard in the distance. When it grew dark the jeeps went on again, and after losing their way, found the rendezvous. Most of the parties had already arrived and the rest came in later. Only Zirnheld, the Frenchman, was killed en route – by the Stukas Stirling had heard firing.

What had the raid achieved? Stirling reckoned that he had destroyed 25 aircraft and damaged a dozen more; and of those destroyed, many were Junkers, each worth several other aircraft, so far as Rommel was concerned. But even this was not the total 'bag', for Lieutenant Wilder of the LRDG had led a diversionary raid against the airfield at Baguish where he destroyed 15 planes. In his report Stirling claimed 40 planes bringing the total for his unit up to 256.

Not unexpectedly the Germans were enraged at their losses in the jeep raid and began sending out motorised columns to hunt for the SAS and LRDG. Stirling had no alternative but to leave his desert base and head east across the Qattara depression. Soon his unit was back at Kabrit and he was reporting to GHQ for new orders.

Daffodil
and other flowers

In August 1942 the situation was static, with the British and German armies facing each other on a 30-mile front at El Alamein. But appearances were deceptive, for both sides were trying to bring up reinforcements in time for the clash anticipated by the end of the month. Allied opinion was that Rommel would attack about the 31st but would be held without great difficulty; and then in October, when the Allies had an overwhelming advantage of men and material, they in turn would move to the attack, and this time Rommel would be driven back once and for all, then destroyed. During this waiting period there had been important changes in the Allied command, Alexander relieving Auchinleck, and Montgomery taking over the 8th Army from Ritchie. With these new commanders came a new air of drive and confidence and the whole Middle East theatre began to hum with plans and activity. This development naturally

had its impact on the small desert units and soon they were advised of a series of operations requiring their specialised services:

1 *Daffodil*: This was an attack on Tobruk to be launched both from land and sea. The object was to capture coastal defence guns, destroy harbour installations and storage tanks which could not be reached from the air.

2 *Snowdrop*: This was to be a raid by Stirling and the SAS against Benghazi, with the object of sinking shipping in the harbour.

3 *Tulip*: This involved the Sudan Defence Force which was to move from Kufra and take Jalo, to provide the SAS with a forward base. Two LRDG patrols would lead the attackers.

4 *Hyacinth*: This operation would be mounted by the LRDG. Two patrols under Easonsmith would cross the sand sea then head for Barce and raid the airfield.

All these operations, as will be seen, were designed to hinder Rommel's communications system and therefore the rapid build-up of his supplies. Tobruk and Benghazi were his main ports and any damage here could have a major impact. It will also be obvious that these operations involved travelling vast distances round the sand seas. The reason was that Rommel had now effectively blocked the entrances to the Qattara depression, and so the old short-cuts were of no use. Again the LRDG's vast experience of the southern areas would prove vital, though whether the immense supply problems could be overcome was a matter of opinion.

Despite the energy with which they were being launched by GHQ many experienced desert hands took a dislike to them from the start. Too many people seemed to be in the know, and talk in the bars and restaurants was sometimes startling. A Free French officer even reported that a barman at his hotel in Beirut (strongly suspected of being a German agent) knew dates, routes, and objectives, even before the raiding parties had set off. However, the Intelligence people at GHQ seemed quite confident, pointing out that the bases would be lightly held by Italian or third-rate German

troops and there was really nothing to worry about.

Stirling never liked the role assigned to him. To begin with he was to lead 220 men, most of them untrained for such an operation; and to transport them and their equipment a transport column would be required totalling 40 trucks and the same number of armed jeeps. How, he argued with the operations staff, could a force of this magnitude achieve surprise – and surprise, as always, was a raider's main weapon. Furthermore, he disliked being tied to such a rigid time-table, much preferring to strike when his instinct told him. As he wrote later, 'The whole plan sinned against every principle on which SAS was founded'. However, during the discussions and arguments at GHQ it became clear that unless he did as requested, his chances of expanding SAS and developing it into the powerful attacking force he wished to see, were nil. So he had no option.

It may be mentioned here that if he disliked the operation against Benghazi, he liked the Tobruk raid even less. The idea had been 'sold' to GHQ by an Arab expert and former secret agent, Colonel John Haselden. Though a man of charm and intelligence, Haselden had never commanded men in action, let alone in a raid. And his operation was to be the largest of all. Escorted by the LRDG he would lead a force of Special Service troops (known as Force B), penetrate the Tobruk perimeter at dusk, and seize an inlet at Mersa Sciausc to the east of the harbour and just outside the boom defence. Once successful here, he would be joined by Force C, 100 men led by Captain McFie of the Argyll and Sutherland Highlanders, brought from Alexandria in Motor Torpedo Boats. Linking up, the combined force would then work their way west, capturing coastal defences and Flak batteries as they came across them. At 0340 hours Force A, drawn from the 11th Battalion Royal Marines, would then land from two destroyers, capture guns to the north of the harbour and enter the town. As a diversion the RAF would bomb Tobruk during the night and as soon as they had left, the MTBs would go in to attack shipping at the east end of the harbour. And when all this had been done demolition parties would land from the destroyers. As will be seen at once, the operation was almost crazy in its complexity, and for success needed perfect co-ordination by air, land and sea, and no hitches of any kind. It also depended on Intelligence at GHQ having got their facts right.

The other operations against Jalo and Barce were less ambitious, but yet again the raiders faced many imponderables, not the least a desert journey of some 1,600 miles.

However, after detailed planning and frantic preparations the opening moves were made. On August 31 – the day Rommel launched his offensive against the 8th Army at El Alamein – David Lloyd Owen and Y patrol of the LRDG led Force B up the Nile from Cairo, then across the bottom of the Great Sand Sea on a five-day journey to Kufra. For the troops in the back of the trucks – most of whom had never seen the desert before – the journey was hot, thirsty, and uncomfortable. The calm assurance of the bearded warriors of the LRDG – the only bearded British soldiers in the Middle East – filled them with awe. It was almost like being taken on a camel ride with Lawrence of Arabia, so great was the legend the patrols had created for themselves. On September 4 the column reached Kufra, which amazed the commandos by its size and the feverish activity going on around it. Two days later they headed north, Lloyd Owen picking his route through the gap between Jalo and the Kalansho Sand Sea. His immediate destination was Hatiet Etla, about a hundred miles from Tobruk, where he knew there was good cover. On September 10 the column arrived there safely. The first 1,500 miles of the outward journey had been accomplished.

By this time Easonsmith with T1 and G1 patrols of the LRDG, was well on the way to Barce. And on the 11th, the Sudan Defence Force left Kufra for their attack on Jalo. This operation, incidentally, was of major importance to the other raiding parties, for if it failed, their escape route might be cut off.

Meanwhile Stirling's force was on the move. He had decided that the only possible route for a column of 80

Not a Bedouin but John Haselden in disguise; he had just herded sheep across an enemy airfield

vehicles was via Bir Zighen which stands at the junction of the two sand seas. The neck joining them is about 20 miles wide, a shifting mass of white sand, forming itself into great ridges and valleys, and across this the column struggled at about one mile an hour. Once past Bir Zighen the journey lay up the western rim of the Kalansho Sand Sea and through the Jalo gap. Stirling, knowing that the garrison at Jalo had radio, passed his column to the east of the town at midday when the heat haze reduced visibility. Three days later they reached the cover of the Jebel mountains; and so far as could be told the enemy had no knowledge of their presence.

Having lagered, Stirling's first job was to locate Bob Melot, the British Agent who lived out with the Arabs, signalling back information whenever he could. Maclean – who was given the job–found him lying up in a *wadi* and after a meal, obtained the latest information. This was not too encouraging. There had been some enemy troop movements, he said, and the impression was that the raid was expected. Deciding to make his own investigations, Stirling went off to

talk with some local sheikhs, and their view also was that the enemy was uneasy about something. The next move was to send someone into Benghazi – an Arab deserter from the Italian Army who had been brought along for such jobs – and the following day, when this individual came back with blistered feet, his story was not exactly cheerful either. Talk in the bazaar, he said, was of a coming attack. Civilians were being evacuated. Italian infantry reinforcements had come in and some German machine-gun detachments. Mines were being laid at approaches to the town. Even the date of the attack was being mentioned.

Faced with this development, Stirling held discussions with Maclean and Melot, and it was decided to signal GHQ asking if plans should be changed. The reply which arrived a few hours later was to continue as planned and keep to the original time-plan. From Cairo the bazaar gossip obviously seemed quite harmless.

So Stirling had no option but to give out his orders. At nightfall the main body would descend the escarpment, motor across the plain to the road, then head towards Benghazi and its harbor at full speed, bursting through any road-blocks which barred the way. By the time this happened, a small party would deal with the Italian radio station at the foot of the escarpment, to prevent its giving warning. To demoralise the enemy and keep them occupied, the RAF had promised to bomb Benghazi for two hours from 2200 hours to 2359 hours. And at midnight, so Stirling hoped, his jeep would just be entering the outskirts of the town.

So things went ahead. After weapons had been checked and every man was equipped with ammunition, a desert escape kit, (which included a silk map of the Western desert, a compass, and a collapsible water bottle), the trucks were loaded up. Chris Bailey and the party detailed to attack the radio station left, and then the main body followed. It was not easy to get the truck down the escarpment as the Arab guide took them along the wrong *wadi*. After some hurried conferences in the dark, it was decided that the route must be abandoned and another found – all of which took a great deal of time. In the distance the bombs could be heard falling on Benghazi. However, once the tarmac road was reached, the column soon formed up and drove

at speed. The delay had not proved so bad as Stirling feared.

Then in the distance a barrier could be seen across the road, flanked by wire. Stopping the column to investigate, Stirling found that the earth had been disturbed to the flanks and suspected the presence of mines. Bill Cumper, the party's expert on mines, was invited to give his opinion, and came forward. After messing around in the darkness for a while, he crawled across to the road-block, and pressing a catch, released the bar so that it flew to an upright position. 'Let battle commence', he remarked cheerfully. Whether he intended the remark literally, it is hard to say, but at this precise moment the enemy, concealed on either side of the road, opened up with machine-guns and 20-mm guns, and within seconds heavy mortars had joined in. The leading truck ran the gauntlet of this curtain of fire, only to receive a bullet in the petrol tank, and the same fate befell the second truck and the third. Meanwhile the rest of the raiding party deployed to their flanks and opened up with every gun they had, with the result that the enemy fire slackened. However, it was obviously a matter of time before reinforcements were called up, and in any case surprise had been lost. There was no option but to withdraw.

Daylight came all too soon, with

There is no substitute for luck: SAS negotiates a minefield. *Below:* **Italian Infantry advancing under fire**

the raiders still at the foot of the escarpment. Here rocky ravines gave some cover, but before concealment was possible the German aircraft were racing out from Benghazi to attack with bombs and machine guns. Their aim was not very accurate, until a lucky shot hit a truck which exploded, marking the target area. As each plane ran out of ammunition it returned to Benghazi to load up again and so at any one moment there were a dozen or more aircraft keeping up the momentum of the attack. Not till the sun went down did they give up.

As soon as possible, Stirling took stock of the position. Several trucks had gone, together with some food and ammunition. Of the party from the radio station, Bob Melot had been badly wounded in the legs, Chris Bailey had a bullet in his lungs, and an NCO had a shattered arm. It was going to be a nasty ride home.

Now we must turn our attention from Snowdrop to Daffodil ... that is from Benghazi to Tobruk. On September 12, while John Haselden and his men had their supper at Hatiet Etla, Force A (Lieutenant-Colonel Unwin, Royal Marines, and 382 officers and men) boarded the destroyers *Sikh* and *Zulu* at Haifa. At Alexandria, Captain MacFie had already got his men aboard the MTBs and they were not very pleased to see their collapsible boats strapped to the outskirts of the lorries, for the whole town to see. Security for the operation continued as bad as ever.

Weather reports for the last twenty-four hours had been depressing, and opinion was among the Met officers that the sea was too rough for landing operations. This view was later confirmed by aerial reconnaissance – but orders from above were that the operation should go ahead as planned.

On the morning of the 6th the desert force moved north from Hatiet Etla to an area where cover was available, some 40 miles from Tobruk, Here they waited, before moving off for the raid in the late afternoon, Haselden's plan being to drive boldly down the main road in four 3-tonners, taking a chance that they would not be identified. Till the main road was in sight, the column was led by David Lloyd Owen and six LRDG trucks,

Daffodil target: Tobruk harbour, north shore

then there was a brief halt for good-byes and Lloyd Owen moved back to the desert. Haselden and his party were on their own now, and his objective lay straight ahead.

The parting had not only been brief but unaccountably sad, quite unlike the partings with Stirling and his men. Though the latter had casualties from time to time, the atmosphere was gay and confident, and everyone knew that they were in good hands. On the Tobruk raid, however, things were quite different. Haselden was no Stirling and everyone knew it. Watching the commandos clambering into their trucks the veterans of the LRDG knew in their hearts that many of them would not see another day.

Apart from Haselden's own inexperience, his second-in-command, Major Campbell, was so sick he could barely walk; instead of taking men into action, he should have been on his way to hospital.

Lloyd Owen did not have long to dally with his thoughts for at this moment he spotted an Italian motorised patrol watching the commando column. Going into action at once, the LRDG trucks roared forward their machine-guns firing, and in a few moments those Italians who were not dead or dying were only too anxious to surrender. Questioning them, Lloyd Owen found that they came from a division which had just moved into Tobruk. The Germans, they added, had also sent reinforcements. Hearing this news Lloyd Owen immediately thought of Haselden and his

party and tried to make radio contact. This proved impossible, and so he had to move away to carry out his own operation, against the RDF station.

Meanwhile Haselden's force had come to the rim of the escarpment at Sidi Resegh, and crawled along it for half an hour before finding a way down. Then there was a bumpy ride towards the Tobruk road, enlivened by the sight of the two German trucks which came heading towards them. But the Germans were uninterested and drove off into the distance. There was a moment of relief, a short moment, for then a reconnaissance plane came from behind the escarpment and, having identified the column, circled it several times at low level, before disappearing in the dusk. Then the trucks bumped a road

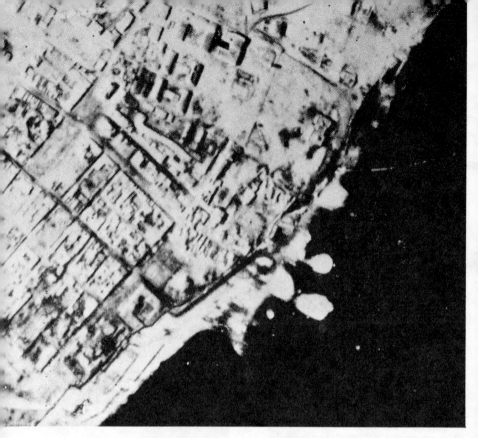

RAF support on the Tobruk raid: *Left:*
Wellington bombers find their target,
Right: aerial photograph taken after
the raid

block, flanked by barbed wire and
sandbag gun emplacements. This was
the Tobruk perimeter. Captain Bray,
dressed as a German officer, and
carrying false documents, leaned forward prepared to talk to the sentries,
but the latter merely smiled and
waved the trucks through. Farther
along they passed a German transport
column, and one of the trucks was hit
a glancing blow by a staff car. There
was a good deal of swearing on both
sides, but the column still went on,
amidst a stream of traffic. On either
side of the road were tented camps,
and individual soldiers or groups of
them could be seen trudging towards
the mess tents for supper, mess tins in
hand. Further down the road, the
German Military Police took an
interest in the column but then went

away without comment. Soon the
trucks were negotiating the second
escarpment dipping into the town
itself. Led by Bray, they turned off the
road, to run along by the sea towards
their immediate objective.

A sentry challenged and the column
came to a halt. Waiting in the trucks
the commandos could see one of their
'German officers' walk into the darkness and there was a tense pause while
the column waited. Then the officer
returned with a German rifle which he
tossed into the truck, remarking
casually that the sentry wouldn't
need it any more. The trucks went on
again but not very far, for this was the
end of the journey, the precise point
on the map they had been heading for
all this time.

Everyone got out and began handing
down equipment. The 'German
officers' hurriedly changed to British
uniform and the whole party got
ready to move off to destroy the guns
covering the harbor. But there was

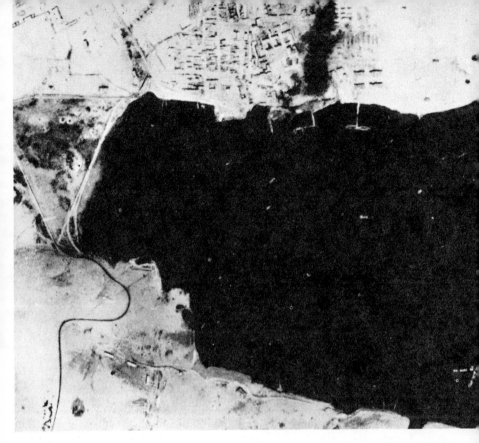

one change of plan: as Campbell was so weak, Haselden asked Langton to go with him and take over if he collapsed. This was a nuisance, as Langton's job was to signal the MTBs when it was ready for them to come in, then to be on the beach to receive them. However, making a rough calculation he decided that he could do both jobs and moved off as ordered. Then a gun began firing at regular intervals. This, as Haselden knew, was the air raid warning.

The RAF came in to the second as planned, and at 2130 hours began to drop their bombs. The commando was on time also and crossing the *wadi* moved silently up the high ground covering Sciausc Bay from the west. Meanwhile Haselden had moved into a villa with his party, taking a group of Italians prisoner, and was now interrogating their NCO about the coastal defence gun sites. How many were there? How many men were on them? How many sentries? Meanwhile, another party of commandos, under Graham Taylor, scrambled up-hill to deal with another gun site, but found it was unguarded. But a second gun site, further along, was crammed with men, and throwing in grenades, Taylor killed the lot of them. From all across the promontory there was heavy firing at first, but whenever they came across opposition the commandos dealt with it, and eventually there was silence. The area was theirs. At midnight the success signal was sent up from a Very light.

But at his headquarters in the captured villa, Haselden was most anxious, for no signal had been received from Major Colin Campbell and his party. Already the MTBs were off shore and ready to land their men but until the signal came, nothing could be done. Increasingly anxious Haselden waited, till 0100 . . . till 0115 hours.

In fact, Campbell's party had been delayed, but when at last they reached their objective, found the gun emplacements empty. Langton immediately asked if he should put up the success signal, two green Very lights, and was told to do so. Meanwhile, Campbell led his men towards their next objective, Brighton Rest Camp, where Intelligence thought there were more guns. Langton now began to carry out his other task, but travelling as fast as he could in the darkness, he realised that if he returned to the Italian villa, where he had left his Aldis lamp, he would never get down to the inlet in time to signal in the MTBs. So he decided that he must use his torch though it was far less powerful. Scrambling down to the inlet, he began signalling – three long flashes every two minutes on a bearing NE and East. He was a little late, but that could not be helped – he couldn't be in two places at once.

But the MTBs did not come in, and from 0130 hours, the time slipped by till 0200 hours . . . and then 0300 hours. Things were going very wrong.

What had happened was that the MTBs had not seen the signal. Also the guiding lights which Haselden's force should have put into position were not there, or were obscured by mist. Eventually, when it was decided to go ahead, only two MTBs found their way into the inlet, and they were greeted by machine-gun fire.

By this time Force A (the destroyers *Sikh* and *Zulu* with the 11th Battalion Royal Marines) had arrived two miles off the coast. Owing to the heavy swell, the party from the submarine *Taku*, whose duty it had been to mark the landing place, could not get ashore, and then some trouble was experienced with the landing-craft improvised for the occasion. By 0500 hours only 70 marines out of 800 had landed and they were two miles west of their correct beach. With great courage this party tried to fight their way into Tobruk, but the task was hopeless and in due course they were overwhelmed. Meanwhile the two destroyers came within a mile of land, searching for the landing-craft which should have returned for the second wave of marines. Immediately shore batteries opened up and *Sikh's* steering gear was put out of action. Though *Zulu* tried to take her on tow, this

The Navy heads for Tobruk: HMS Coventry

proved impossible, for the cable was cut by a shell, and both ships were hit again and again. Eventually *Zulu* had to put to sea and *Sikh* was scuttled, both her own company and the marines aboard her being forced to surrender as prisoners of war. As daylight approached the enemy brought in fighter-bombers and dive-bombers from airfields along the coast and from Crete, and at 1115 hours an anti-aircraft cruiser steaming to help *Zulu*, was hit by bombs and sank. *Zulu*, hounded by the enemy from sea and air, limped her way back to Alexandria. Apart from the two MTBs which had entered the inlet at Mersa Sciausc, and had to be abandoned, three others were sunk by enemy action. So far as the naval element was concerned, the Tobruk raid had proved disastrous.

From the army viewpoint it had proved no better, and long before these gallant ships went down, John Haselden, the architect of the raid, was dead.

He knew that the game was up when the MTBs failed to come in on cue, but so long as there was a chance, it

was his duty to hold on to the bridge-head. Nothing had been heard from Colin Campbell for five hours, and runners had been sent to try and contact them. Out at sea he could see the Royal Navy trying and failing to fulfill its task, the MTBs coming towards the shore in waves, to be picked up by the searchlights then harassed by the guns.

When daylight came, it found Haselden and what was left of his party gathered round the villa which had been his headquarters. Enemy activity was increasing from all sides, and it was with little surprise that officers and men heard him say, 'I'm sorry, chaps, but this is the end. It's every man for himself.' At this moment parties were blowing up German guns, dodging from emplacement to emplacement under heavy fire. Some were killed, but others racing back to the villa reported that tanks and armored cars were moving against them. At this moment a message arrived from Campbell – he had encountered heavy resistance; many of his party were wounded and he himself had been shot through the thigh.

It was time to go. A group of officers put the wounded into a truck with the wild idea of making a dash for the perimeter, but before they got away a message came that a party of the enemy were in position on the *wadi* intending to ambush the truck as it came in view. Immediately two SIG officers and some of their men dashed down the slope to deal with the situation, and found Haselden there ahead of them. With his tommy-gun he had taken on ten Italians, and was giving a very good account of himself, moving forward from cover to cover. Then the truck came round and Haselden, seeing a threatening move from the Italians, charged towards them firing his gun till he ran out of ammunition. The truck got through. But meanwhile enemy reinforcements had come up and fire was sweeping across the ground from many angles. Haselden was hit and could be seen quite still lying face downwards. Gallantly two men of the SIG tried to get to him and then a Scottish subaltern called MacDonald who raced across the open ground under fire. But then a stick bomb came curving through the air, to land on Haselden's back, and when the smoke had cleared there was nothing left of him.

From now on there was little con-

HMS Coventry is hit and sinking

certed action. It was a matter of officers and men running hither and thither, trying to find cover from fire, trying to hit the enemy whenever opportunity presented itself, trying to get away. But no one thought of surrender, and the little party by the villa still held off large numbers of enemy enduring heavy mortar fire as well as machine-gun fire. But eventually their ammunition ran out, and trying to move away, they bumped into a German battalion. There was no alternative but to put their hands up.

When night closed in again only ten men were still alive and uncaptured. David Lanark was with Private Weiz-

mann and a commando, Private Watler, and they were making their way along the coast to a point where they hoped a submarine or MTB would pick them up. David Langton was with Sergeant Evans and Corporal Steiner of the Commandos, and four men. Between the seven of them they had some biscuits, cheese, chocolate, and about four pints of water. Both parties had got through the perimeter and were heading east towards their own lines. Their journey went on for weeks. Occasionally they met Arabs who gave them water and food but their numbers decreased. One of Langton's party got lost. Then Sergeant Evans began suffering so badly from dysentery that there was no alternative for him but to surrender

and get medical treatment. Private Weizmann was shot, trying to break into an Italian camp to get food. The other soldier went down with dysentery. Langton had only three men with him now. And on November 13 they got home. Five days later a British armored car saw what looked like the skeleton of a British officer, walking through the desert. He was bearded and in rags, but he had the strength to say, 'I am Lieutenant David Lanark'.

Snowdrop. . . Daffodil. . . It is now the turn of Tulip, the attack on Jalo by the Sudan Defence Force. Leaving Kufra on September 11, as already recorded, the party reached Jalo on the night of the 15th/16th. Halting 15 miles off the three columns advanced on foot, each guided by an officer of the LRDG. Nothing was seen till they were within 100 yards of the village and fort, but then the Italian sentries challenged and it was quite obvious that they were alert and waiting. Deploying rapidly, the columns went into the attack, and succeeded in getting into the north fort. But all the time the enemy seemed to be getting stronger and the position was lost, and confused fighting went on all night. For the next four days, the attackers held a position by the western edge of the oasis, where they shelled the fort and were bombarded themselves in turn. Between the bursts of action, the Arabs crawled among the weapon pits selling eggs and chickens. By the morning of the 20th GHQ had come to the conclusion that the operation had no chance of success whatever, and called it off. So the Sudan Defence Force made its way back to Kufra, having accomplished nothing.

Three flowers had withered. Only Hyacinth, Jake Easonsmith's raid on Barce was left and nothing had been heard of them for days. Was there a fourth failure to be recorded? No. In spite of appalling difficulties, Hyacinth at least had blossomed into flower.

On September 10 Easonsmith and his two patrols, T 1 and G 1 came to the edge of the Great Sand Sea. Ahead lay 200 miles of the country that they knew so well, and they pushed across it with vigour, till reaching a point 15 miles short of Barce. Here Major Peniakoff (later to become famous as 'Popski') who had accompanied the force, was dropped off with two of his Arab tribesmen, with the task of finding out what they could about the garrison. They would meet the force again as it moved forward after dark. Of Easonsmith's patrols, incidentally, G 1 – the Guardsmen – were commanded by Captain J A L Timpson and T 1 – the New Zealanders – by Captain Nick Wilder. During the afternoon they made their usual preparations, then after dark set off, hitting the Gerdes el 'Abid track and turning northwards, having cut the telephone wires. At Sidi Raui a soldier came out of the police post to challenge, and Easonsmith's action

After the bomber raid: smoke rises from Tobruk harbour

was to blind him with the headlamps, then disarm him and bundle him into the truck. When there was movement in the police post, Easonsmith called out in Arabic: Ta'ala henna, Ta'ala henna. (Come here! Come here!) and as an Italian officer appeared, shot him dead. The remainder of the Italians clambered away over the back wall of the post. Five miles further on at Sidi Selim Major Peniakoff was waiting, but his Arabs had not returned. Here Lawson was left behind with the wireless truck, to form a rallying point, and the remainder of the men headed towards the main road, then turned westwards.

Five miles from Barce two Italian tanks had taken up positions covering the road, but fortunately they were deceived by the headlights into thinking the LRDG trucks were an Italian column. Too late they found themselves under heavy fire from the fast moving trucks which soon disapeared down the road.

At the crossroads outside the town, the force split up. Peniakoff stayed behind to deal with any pursuers; Wilder and T 1 turned right for the airfield; the Guards headed for the barracks; and Easonsmith drove to-

Knocked-out guns at Tobruk. *Below:* **Destruction in Tobruk harbour**

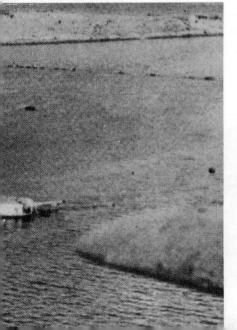

wards the town on his own errand. Wilder soon reached the main gate of the airfield, opened it, and drove in, shooting down some Italians who ran forward to oppose him. His column now consisted of a Jeep and four 30-cwt trucks and he led it round the mess buildings and offices, hurling grenades, then turned towards the landing strip. Here were parked lines of aircraft which were treated to bursts of incendiary fire, and any which did not start burning were set off by bombs thrown from the last truck. By the time the column turned away again, 20 aircraft were burning and the rest were seriously damaged. Though a good deal of fire was coming from the Italians, it was ill-directed and did no damage. His ammunition running low, Wilder led the patrol away from the airfield.

The Guards were now under Sergeant Dennis, Captain Timpson having been injured when his Jeep overturned, and when the New Zealanders had turned right for the airfield, they had gone straight ahead. Later he wrote:

'We soon found the barracks. A dozen or more soldiers had gathered on the low verandah in front of the building, curious to find out the cause of all the noise. As we passed I tossed a grenade among them. Men on the trucks behind gave them one each, and a series of rapid explosions enlivened the party.'

'I carried on as far as I could up the side of the building. Duncalfe emptied his twins (Vickers K guns) into the windows of the barracks as we swept past and the other guns picked out other windows for attention. In the meantime the Breda gun was pumping shells through the front door of the building. Screams and yells mingled with the sound of furniture came from inside the barracks and I called for my gunners to cease firing and to reload.'

Dennis then led his men in an attempt to scale the wall but was prevented by some troops who had got out of the buildings and into slit trenches. Then the enemy brought up tanks and for a moment it looked as if the column was trapped, until Dennis found a gap in the boundary wall and led his column through this. After dealing with some more

Captive in the sun

Italian infantry attacking

buildings, the patrol got away, to meet Wilder and his truck. The New Zealander was hit, but seemed more concerned about three wounded men he had aboard. Leaving the airfield, his column bumped some tanks on the road, and racing away from them his Jeep had been overturned. Wilder was pinned underneath, but as soon as the men freed him got back into the driving seat, picked up some wounded and drove on.

Meanwhile, Easonsmith had been shooting up buildings, taking on two tanks, attacking a party of troops with grenades, then wrecking transport.

By 0400 hours he decided it was time to withdraw and collect his forces, and despite the hectic activity they had been engaged in, the two patrols met him at Sidi Selim, ten vehicles being left out of the 12 which had gone into Barce. So they began the journey home in the dark, the six wounded men travelling in the last truck with the doctor. Some miles along the track entered a narrow valley and as the column reached this in the half light, firing broke out on

either side, the Italians evidently having laid an ambush. Several men were wounded immediately and the doctor's car received a bullet in the tyre. Without hesitation, Sergeant Dennis turned his truck round to give him cover, while the wheel was changed. Then as the trucks moved forward he circled them blazing away with his guns at anything that moved. In time the firing ceased.

A few miles further on the column stopped to brew up tea and attempt repairs to three trucks which were now on tow. While this was happening, some of the troops from the ambush came forward to attack once more with rifles and machine-guns. Leaping into his jeep Easonsmith headed towards them with his gunner firing the Vickers. Before long the enemy had had enough, and having let off smoke grenades, retired through the scrub.

This minor action had wasted time, and it was broad daylight. Expecting the bombers to arrive at any moment, Easonsmith decided to blow up the three lame trucks and push on with the rest. Seven miles further on the wireless truck broke down – and worse still, the party was spotted by a reconnaissance plane. At 1030 hours

the fighters arrived and from now till dusk the attack continued. The only cover was some low scrub, and there was no protection from fire. By evening only one 30-cwt truck and two Jeeps were left to take 33 men on the 800-mile journey to Kufra, and by now several more were wounded. Easonsmith gave out his orders: Lawson would leave for Bir Gerrari and Kufra in a Jeep and 30-cwt with six wounded men, a driver, fitter, and Davis as navigator. Two walking parties with a jeep for food and water would head for the same destination.

Some time during the night, the Jeep with the walking party had a hole knocked in the sump by a rock and two hours were lost repairing it. Next day the party pushed on and at night found an Arab encampment where they bought a lamb to cook and milk to drink. On the 16th they were lucky to find water. And just before dawn on the 17th they heard cars passing which they were sure must belong to their own unit, but although they fired Very lights, the cars went on. But an hour later the party topped a rise to find Olivey and his Rhodesians encamped in a hollow and cooking breakfast.

Lawson and his party reached their rendezvous and were flown back to Cairo by the RAF. Of the LRDG casualties all recovered. Ten men were taken prisoners of war. 14 vehicles were lost. Easonsmith and Wilder were awarded DSOs; and an MC and three MMs were handed out. Later the Italians reported 16 aircraft destroyed and 7 damaged 'by British armoured cars'.

To complete this story it is necessary to go back to Stirling, Maclean, and their party, who it may be remembered, we left at the base of the escarpment, having been hammered all day by fighters and bombers. By the light of the blazing trucks they divided up the available food and water and split into three parties, under Stirling, Mayne, and Maclean respectively. Chris Bailey and the more seriously wounded men were sent towards Benghazi with an Italian prisoner under a Red Cross Flag, and the rest including Bob Melot went with the escaping columns.

It was a dark night and the going was slow. The plan was to make for the Jebel and get into cover there, then lie up for the whole day. Maclean's party was lucky, finding a *wadi* just before daylight, where it was possible

Off load, change tyre, re-load

to conceal the trucks and hide in the scrub. Some time in the morning Maclean and Alston looked across the desert to see a squadron of enemy aircraft attacking another column, and then there was a column of smoke, indicating that one or more trucks had been hit. In fact, these belonged to Stirling's column, his hiding place having been given away by an SAS driver who had become detached the night before and was now heading to rejoin the party. By the time the raid was over, Stirling calculated that 20 men would have to ride in each 3-tonner and eight in each jeep. Worse still there was only enough petrol as far as Jalo. Fervently he hoped that the Sudan Defence Force had captured it.

Next morning the parties pressed on. Maclean experienced difficulty in finding his way out of the complex of *wadis* but eventually was on the open desert. Here the progress was much faster but dawn came up with no shred of cover in sight, except for some scrub about 18 inches high. Dispersing the trucks, the men put the nets over and broke off twigs, to help break the line. Then they found holes in the sand and tried to sleep, heavily attacked by the flies. Luckily, however, these were the only enemy to appear throughout the day; not an aircraft was seen in the sky.

Next night the column went on again, and throughout the following day, the risk of detection from the air having to be taken because of the shortage of food and water. It was mercilessly hot, and sometimes men would doze off and fall from the trucks which would then halt till they could clamber on again. By sunset on September 18 the columns were about 30 miles from Jalo, and had a much better evening meal, trusting that they would get supplies next morning.

At midnight Maclean left to make a reconnaissance towards the oasis to find out whether the enemy were there or the Sudanese. Very lights which were sent up as a recognition signal produced no reply, so the party waited till dawn before heading towards the palm trees. Three German planes came over and dropped a stick of bombs, which seemed to indicate that the Sudanese must still be around, and this impression was reinforced when some guns opened up and began shelling the Italian fort at the centre of the town. Then shells began coming towards Maclean and his party and he began to realise that he was in the midst of a battle. Moving away swiftly, he was able to make contact with the SDF and learned that they had been in action for five days. Moreover, they had just received a signal from GHQ ordering them to withdraw to Kufra.

However, all was not lost. The SDF gladly provided food and petrol, there was plenty of water in the wells, and the palm trees were heavy with dates. By now Stirling and Mayne had arrived with their parties, and soon the columns were heading south towards Kufra. Their anxieties were by no means over: GHQ in its signals to the SDF had indicated that the SAS had diverted considerable numbers of German troops from the front; armored columns and infantry were scouring the desert for them; aircraft had been put on the job. Though this attention was flattering, and it was better to have GHQ's approbation than disapproval, the men had a naked, helpless feeling as the desert stretched bare before them. So to put more miles between them and the pursuing enemy, they went on through the next night, using headlights. Dawn found them in what Maclean has described as 'a kind of desert archipelago', great cliffs rearing up from the sand, crowned with grass, shrubs, and trees. This was an ideal hiding place and the column concealed itself and lay up during the whole day. Next night they went on again and the following day, hitting an ancient caravan trail which led to Zighen and the oasis of Bir Harash. The SDF column was already encamped here, and pointed out wells with a supply of blackish water.

From now on the journey went on without major incident though unsticking the trucks in the Sand Sea was a long wearisome business. Two days later, with the trucks breaking down every mile or so, the column crept into Kufra just before dark. The men had only one desire – sleep, hours and hours of uninterrupted sleep. And this desire they were granted.

Corporal, LRDG

Desert rendezvous. What has happened to the others?

El Alamein
and after

Arriving back in Cairo early in October Stirling found that Montgomery had set up a new department called 'G Raiding Force', under Colonel Shan Hackett, and soon it became clear that the SAS would come under this. Fortunately, on meeting Hackett, Stirling took a liking to him, and discussed plans for his unit during the coming offensive. What the SAS should be doing, he argued, was to cause chaos in Rommel's rear, harass his line of communications, hinder his withdrawal by raids every night. Such a programme, naturally, would need many more men, and these would have to be already acclimatised and from good units. Hackett, appreciating the point, arranged an appointment with Montgomery in person, and the two Colonels went to see him in his caravan. Immediately it was apparent that Montgomery shared the regular officer's contempt for irregular units to the full; and Stirling's tremendous achievements in the past two years

meant nothing to him. He even taunted Stirling with his failure at Benghazi. On his side, Stirling laughed at Montgomery's calm assurance that he would smash Rommel's army once and for all, pointing out that a succession of generals had promised to do this and failed. The upshot was that Montgomery refused permission for the SAS to recruit from regiments; all it could have were men from the Infantry Base Depot, most of them straight out from home. And with this Stirling had to be content.

On October 23 Montgomery opened his offensive at El Alamein and after four days of savage and costly fighting broke through Rommel's line and pushed him right back to Agheila. Here the 8th Army paused again for a month, and Montgomery had to lay on another offensive, for although Rommel had been badly mauled, his army was still in being and full of fight.

During this interval, Stirling went on recruiting whatever men he could find, and though Montgomery disliked him, Alexander (the latter's superior) and Winston Churchill were full of admiration. So it was arranged that the SAS should take over not only the Special Boat Section but what remained of the Middle East Commando. All told, he now had about 800 men.

But what was the SAS to do as the 8th Army moved forward? Stirling put up a plan, the gist of which was that he should make movement along the coastal road so difficult at night that the Germans would have to move by day, so exposing themselves to the RAF. This plan was agreed by Montgomery, and so a base was reconnoitred in a *wadi* called Bir Zalten, about 150 miles south of Agheila. From here Stirling planned to send out so many raiding parties that the road would virtually be under attack from Agheila in the east to Tripoli in the west – a distance of 400 miles. The administrative and operational difficulties were, of course, enormous, but Stirling was quite confident he could bring things off. Even Montgomery was impressed and is said to have remarked, 'The Boy Stirling is mad. Quite, quite mad. Who but him could think of such a plan? Yet if it comes off I don't mind saying it could

Rommel: he paid tribute to the desert raiders

have a decisive effect, yes, a really decisive effect on my forthcoming offensive.' Hearing this, Hackett signalled Stirling, 'Army Commander feels your activities could have decisive effect on course of battle.' To which Stirling replied, 'Congratulate Army Commander on perspicacity.'

Stirling and his command had left Kabrit on November 20 and a week later was safely installed in his base behind the enemy lines. There was ample information as to what was happening on the coastal road, for the LRDG were already on road watch, recording details of every single vehicle which passed along. Timpson, now recovered from his injuries, led the Guards patrol on a brilliant operation, keeping the road under observation for 15 days at a stretch before being relieved and returning to Kufra. The day that he arrived there, December 13, saw the opening of Montgomery's offensive and the start of Stirling's operation. Stirling put two squadrons on the job 'A' and 'B', each divided into eight patrols of three jeeps, and each jeep carrying three men. The orders were that each patrol should deliver an attack on the road

every three days; they would choose their own objectives, blowing up transport, cutting telephone wires, and putting down mines.

Unfortunately, Stirling could not stay to direct operations, as Hackett demanded his presence back at Kabrit, where administrative decisions had to be taken. Undoubtedly his genius was missed and one by one the patrols came to grief, though each managed to make two or three raids first. Stirling, who had hoped to continue for weeks on end, was disappointed, but – as can be seen now – he succeeded better than he knew. In his diary Rommel wrote of the many sabotage raids, and

knew precisely who was behind them. One of his entries reads as follows:

'On the 23rd December we set off at 1700 hours on a beautiful sunny morning to inspect the country south of our front. First we drove along the Via Balbia and then – with two Italian armoured cars as escort – through the fantastically fissured wadi Zem-Zem towards El Fascia. Soon we began to find the tracks made by some of Stirling's people who had been round there on the job of harassing our supply traffic.'

Naturally Rommel gave orders that the raiders should be hunted down by all means possible and by the beginning of January the game was over. Out of all the officers in 'B' Squadron, only three remained uncaptured. 'A' Squadron commanded by Paddy Mayne had been allocated the stretch of road between Agheila and Buerat, but before they could carry out many raids, GHQ signalled them to stop, as the 8th Army was bursting through. Stirling had no alternative but to call his patrols back and re-group for whatever new tasks could be found for them.

By now, as he realised, the whole atmosphere of the Middle East Theatre had changed dramatically. Alexander and Montgomery were not just two more generals as he had rashly assumed; they were superb commanders and knew just what they were up to. Moreover they had now achieved a massive material superiority over Rommel and meant to employ it with the utmost ruthlessness not only to drive the Afrika Korps back towards Tunisia, but to destroy it. Everywhere the troops were brimming over with confidence. Also, of course, an Allied Army under Eisenhower had landed in Algeria, behind Rommel's back and was pushing south and east. At last victory was in sight.

Montgomery's next push was timed for January 15 and with this he hoped to reach a point well beyond Tripoli. The tasks given to the SAS, to tie in with this operation, were as follows: Captain Jordan and three Free French patrols would raid the line of communications between Sfax and Gabes in Tunisia, and a second force would make a demonstration to the west of Tripoli, while the 8th Army attacked from the east and south. The object of this demonstration was to create panic so that the Germans retreated before destroying installations. A third force of the SAS was given the job of reconnoitring the Mareth Line in Tunisia, 200 miles west of Tripoli; and Stirling himself would carry out a reconnaissance in Northern Tunisia and link up with the British First Army.

For this mission Stirling decided to take Sadler as navigator, for the job of traversing the unknown territory of Algeria was obviously going to be a tricky one. He set out on January 10, making for Bir Guedaffia, where he was joined by Jordan and his three patrols. It was now decided to split into two sections, which would travel independently to a rendezvous in North Tunisia called Bir Soltane. This was in the territory that Stirling had to reconnoitre for 8th Army Intelligence, and would make a good jumping-off point for Jordan and his operations between Sfax and Gabes.

At first the going was good and the trucks cruised along at 50 mph till they reached Ghadames. Here they learned that General Leclerc and the Free French forces, now making their brilliant march from Lake Chad, were only 70 miles away.

There was no time to greet them, however, and Stirling turned north through an area known as 'the Great Sea Ergh', the most frightful ground to negotiate he had ever experienced. Near Bir Soltane he moved off to reconnoitre the country around the Mareth line, and here learned that Montgomery had taken Tripoli. In the same signal, 8th Army Intelligence urgently requested that raids should be carried out on Sfax and Gabes as quickly as possible. Stirling ordered Jordan and his column north at once, and also reconsidered his own schedule. His route to Algiers and the First Army would normally have run to the south of Lake Djerid, but in view of the 8th Army's rapid advance he decided to cut down his reconnaissance to a day and follow Jordan through the gap between the lake and coastline at Gabes ('the Gabes Gap') and hurry north to attack Sousse before going on. Intelligence information was that Rommel's supply position was growing desperate, and every blow at his rear helped the 8th Army considerably.

So Stirling hurried north, over difficult country towards the Gap. With him he had five Jeeps and 14 men. Just before dusk two German reconnaissance planes appeared and after circling round, spotted the column and flew off again.

What had happened, Stirling reckoned, was that Jordan had begun his operations and the Germans were keeping a careful watch on the Gap. Quite obviously ground forces would be alerted and start heading towards him, and so it was imperative to get through the Gap before daylight. Painfully the column struggled on, along rocky paths, cut by deep ravines, and by daylight had covered a further 20 miles. Now they found themselves on the edge of the Gafsa road and could see the enemy traffic moving along it. Waiting an hour before till the path was clear, they dashed across and drove northwards another 20 miles till a deep *wadi* offered excellent cover. Having hidden the vehicles, Stirling

The captors are German: the prisoners are British. *Below:* **The column will move at dawn . . .**

Tunisia – scene of the final act of the desert drama

Above: Patrol stops to search a small fort

Below: Beards are not worn in Cairo: Guy Prendergast and two of his men

Victory at El Alamein: the guards are New Zealanders, the prisoners are German

sent Sadler and another officer to have a look round, and before long they were reporting that there was another road about a mile ahead full of enemy traffic. There was also some sort of depot, with trucks loading and unloading. Taking the news calmly Stirling suggested that everyone had a good sleep. The following night they would raid Sousse.

But things went wrong. About teatime Sadler and Cooper at the entrance to the *wadi* heard the noise of army boots and found themselves facing armed troops. The raiders had been caught napping. Stirling, who had been asleep in a cave, awoke to find a revolver pointed at him by a soldier who looked distinctly frightened. Backing out of the cave, the soldier motioned Stirling to follow him, and there seemed no option but

to obey. Blinking at the daylight, Stirling looked up to see the rim of the *wadi* lined with troops, their guns pointing down at him, hundreds of them. At last, at long last, his luck had run out.

The prisoners were allowed to collect their personal gear then were rounded up and put into a lorry. After a two-hour journey, they pulled up at a camp which seemed to be near Medina. Already Stirling was planning to escape and, when darkness came, he asked to be taken to the toilet, then made a bolt with another officer called McDermott. The plan, crude as it was, seemed to work, and Stirling got six hundred yards away to some bushes without being hit. Failing to find McDermott he covered 15 miles during the hours of darkness and found a large Arab house whose owner seemed glad to see him and produced food and drink. That day Stirling lay in a barn. By his reckoning he was 30 miles from Bir Soltane and could cover 20 of them before dawn. In fact, he delayed an hour to reconnoitre a nearby airfield full of Junkers 52s, and then found the country so difficult that he barely covered ten miles. Finding a small ravine he lay down to sleep, being awakened just before sunset the following evening by an Arab, who offered food and drink. Following him down the *wadi* Stirling walked right into the trap prepared for him. Suddenly the Arab pulled out a gun, and looking ahead Stirling saw five truckloads of troops, bristling with machine-guns.

There was no getting away this time. The Phantom Major was a phantom no longer.

Though Stirling's capture created confusion in the SAS this was not the end of the unit. Paddy Mayne took over and as the war progressed to Italy, France, and Germany, no less than five regiments were formed, two British, two French, and one Belgium. They did great work, but the desert was now behind them. The achievements of the desert raiders were now history.

With the Allied advance the LRDG finished its work and the trucks rode back to Cairo for the last time. In January and February the main task of the unit had been to explore thousands of square miles of territory to the south of the Mareth line, and the following month this great effort was rewarded. Studying the LRDG reports, Montgomery decided that it was possible to outflank the line, and detailed the New Zealand division for the job. To move such a large body of men through the desert meant the creation of dumps and it was the LRDG's job to choose the locations and guide the supply trucks to them. By mid-March all was ready and the route marked out. On the 19th, led by LRDG navigators, the division moved towards Gebel Tabaqa with El Hamma and Gabes as the final objectives. Sensing the threat, Rommel moved a Panzer division and two infantry divisions west of Gabes to plug the gap; but Montgomery in turn reinforced the New Zealanders with the 1st Armoured Division, supported in force by the RAF and USAF. These forces inflicted a heavy defeat on the Germans and Rommel was forced to abandon his line and pull back. Four days after Gabes fell, Montgomery wrote to Prendergast, as commander of the LRDG:

'My Dear Prendergast,

We are sending back the Indian Long Range Squadron tomorrow. They have done some useful jobs here – road recces, protective patrols for aerodromes, etc. but I feel that there will be no further scope for them in the country we are now entering.

'I would like you to know how much I appreciate the excellent work done by your patrols and by the SAS in reconnoitring the country up to the Gabes Cap.

'Without your careful and reliable reports the launching of the 'left hook' by the New Zealand Division would have been a leap in the dark; with the information they produced the operation could be planned with some certainty and, as you know, went off without a hitch.

'Please give my thanks to all concerned and best wishes from Eighth Army for the new tasks you are undertaking.

Yours sincerely,
B. L. Montgomery.'

Being a prisoner of war, Stirling was denied the comfort of such signals. Had he known it, however, he might have drawn some satisfaction from the entry made by Field-Marshal Rommel in his diary at this time. 'Thus the British lost the very able and adaptable commander of the desert group which had caused us more damage than any other British unit of equal strength.'

At 1316 hours on May 13, General Alexander signalled the Prime Minister, Winston Churchill: 'Sir, it is my duty to report that the Tunisian campaign is over. All enemy resistance has ceased. We are masters of the North African shores. I now await your further commands.' The victory had taken three years, many battles, and much sacrifice; of the formations engaged, the desert raiders of the LRDG and SAS formed numerically a minute part. But it is true to say that without their efforts victory would have come later and a far greater cost. Their role in the history of warfare remains unique.

Bibliography

Tobruk Commando Gordon
Landsborough (Cassell 1956)
The Long Range Desert Group W B
Kennedy-Shaw (Collins 1945)
G Patrol M Crichton-Stuart (Kimber
1958)
Eastern Approaches Fitzroy Maclean
(Cape 1949)
The Phantom Major Virginia Cowles
(Collins 1958)
Born of the Desert Malcolm James
(Collins 1945)
The Mediterranean and Middle East
Vols III and IV. History of the Second
World War. (HMSO)
Rommel Desmond Young (Collins 1950)